Angels, Masters, & Guides

Angels, Masters, & Guides

How to Work with Them to Heal & to Accelerate Your Spiritual Evolution

GINA LAKE

Endless Satsang Foundation

www.RadicalHappiness.com

Cover photo: © Healing63/Depositphotos.com

ISBN: 979-8379178710

Copyright © 2023 by Gina Lake

All rights reserved. No part of this book may be used or reproduced by any means, graphic, electronic, or mechanical, including photocopying, recording, taping, or by any information storage retrieval system without the written permission of the publisher except in the case of brief quotations embodied in critical articles and reviews.

CONTENTS

Introduction · vii

CHAPTER 1 Who You Are and Where You Came From · 1

CHAPTER 2 Working with Angels · 13

What Angels Do and How to Work with Them — Clearing Entities

CHAPTER 3 Freeing Yourself from Negative Emotions · 35

Being with Difficult Feelings — Replacing Negative Beliefs with Positive Ones — Working with the Inner Child

CHAPTER 4 Working with Ascended Masters and Guides · 51

How to Connect with Ascended Masters and Guides — The Practice of Prayer — Why Prayer Is Healing — What You Receive When You Pray — How Guides Use Signs and Symbols to Guide You — A Guided Meditation for Meeting Your Guide and Receiving Guidance

CHAPTER 5 What Physical Healing Is All About   81

How Physical Issues Serve the Soul--Transmissions

CHAPTER 6 Meditation   109

The Benefits of Meditation—How to Meditate—Overcoming Resistance to Meditation—Inquiries to Overcome Resistance to Meditation

CHAPTER 7 Spiritual Practices Important to Healing   125

The Practice of Forgiveness—Gratitude Practice—A Practice of Focusing on Positive States—The Practice of Smiling—The Practice of Sending Love—More About the Practice of Sending Love—A Guided Meditation for Experiencing Who You Are

About the Author   145

Introduction

I am the one you have known as Jesus the Christ. In this book, I explain what angels, Ascended Masters, and guides are and how to develop a relationship with them that will be healing on all levels. You will also be given practical steps you can take to support your own healing, such as meditation, how to work with difficult emotions and clear negativity, and various key spiritual practices that will also help you heal so that you can live your best life as the loving and divine being that you truly are.

Those who are involved with you from other dimensions are but a tiny fraction of beings who exist in other dimensions. The ones you know of and are familiar with, such as myself, have taken on the task of serving humanity specifically. That is our focus and how we are choosing to advance our own evolution, for everyone is evolving spiritually on every dimension. Everyone is teaching and everyone is learning, even on higher dimensions. Evolution is built into life on every level.

In this book, I hope to convey the immensity of the creation and the immensity of love that beings on higher dimensions have for humanity, for we view you as our very own selves and our beloveds. This may be hard for you to believe, as you are ensconced in a reality where you feel quite separate and apart from each other and from the Creator, but that is the illusion you are here to see through.

In coming to Earth, you have taken on a challenge, and that challenge is to come to see yourself truly, as you truly are—as we see you. Your soul freely chose this challenge because it understands that earthly lifetimes offer a unique and powerful opportunity, unlike anywhere else in creation, to evolve spiritually and, particularly, to increase your capacity to love.

This may sound contradictory: To increase your capacity to love, you came to a place where you are challenged to love. But that is how this is done. Before true love can be known and appreciated, you need to experience what it's like to not feel love and not be loved. In your earthly lifetimes, you're exploring the absence of love in order to get to the fullness of love. These lifetimes change your soul forevermore, as they leave an imprint that shapes and informs all experiences that follow.

There is so much I want to share with you about the immensity and profundity of life, and I will do my best to do so in this book. Your ability to comprehend and realize this is limited, however, by the very things that make you uniquely human: your mind, body, and intellect. These make up your soul's physical vehicle, and this vehicle is a limited one, as it must be. Nevertheless, these limitations provide the soul with a particular experience of life that it couldn't have anywhere else, and that makes these lifetimes very precious.

One of the limitations built into this vehicle is an inability to recall your true nature and your greatness. Being human is like being squeezed into a shoe that's too tiny. The vehicle you find yourself in constricts you, limits you, hurts you, and distorts your perceptions to the point that you've forgotten your origins and are primarily aware of yourself as the character you've come here to play. But that is as it's meant to be, for how could you play this character fully and believably if you remembered who you really are and where you came from?

And yet, there comes a time in everyone's evolution to awaken out of being this character and discover who you really are. That's why you are reading or listening to this now. It's time for you to realize your true nature and discover what is really going on in this human life. It's time for you to discover the Truth, with a capital "T." I'm writing this to help you discover this and to explain the Truth to you so that you can begin to live more fully and freely as the loving and divine being that you are. If that sounds good, then let's begin by exploring who you really are and where you came from...

Chapter 1
Who You Are and Where You Came From

There was no beginning to what you call God or Source, and there will be no end to creation. God/the Creator is infinitely expanding and exploring every possibility through creation. Your mind cannot begin to comprehend the nature of creation and all that exists, but I will do my best to express what needs to be understood by you, which will, hopefully, better enable you to live your best life here in this strange place called Earth.

I say "strange," in part, because Earth is unique to all of creation. There is no other place in creation exactly like it, and there are no other human beings exactly like yourselves. This place is strange in another way, however: It is a place where all that matters is love, and yet, love is apparently quite absent at times. You want love and you know love, and yet, people act as if they don't hold love as the highest value.

Your nature is contradictory, or so it seems. This is because you are divided: Your true nature is love, and you know this on some level, while your programming creates a "false nature," or false self, that places other values above love, such as wealth, prestige, power, success, and being right. You are at war within yourselves. What will win out? Love or power? Kindness or selfishness? Peace or war? Even the most high-minded and spiritually evolved people struggle to be their best selves at times.

This is not an easy situation you find yourselves in! And yet, you chose it—your soul chose to come here to develop more love. Love is the Creator's nature, and love is limitless, so the Creator finds ways to further expand itself through love. Just as you might lift weights to strengthen your muscles, the Creator (through you, through your soul) takes on some heavy lifting here on Earth to become stronger.

This makes sense, doesn't it? On Earth (and in many other places), this is how it works: If you need to develop a talent or skill, you have to work at it. You start out with little talent or skill and you develop it through effort.

This is not to say that effort of this nature is required in every dimension and location within creation. There are some places that could be called "resting places," where little effort is required and all needs are provided for. But to eternal beings such as yourselves, that sort of "heaven" becomes uninteresting fairly quickly. It turns out that if you want an interesting and expanding experience, you need a challenge and you need effort to overcome that challenge. And so it is on Earth and in many other places.

Your soul welcomes this challenge because it chose it. And if it chooses to rest afterwards, it will do that. But for now, while you're on Earth, it's safe to assume that your soul willingly and enthusiastically chose the challenges it's experiencing on every level. To conclude otherwise would be to impede your progress, and the point is to progress and overcome such challenges, including any negative or defeatist attitudes. Being on Earth is a little like being at boot camp, in that you're being trained to be tough, strong, courageous, patient, responsible, persevering, accepting, and also loving and kind. That's a tall order, to be all of those things at once! But that's the challenge your soul has taken on.

Your soul's intention is to become your best self, and your soul will take as long as it needs to, to become that. Being successful, for instance, without also being your best self in the highest sense of the word—your loving, courageous, and kind self—will not lead to satisfaction in the end. And being powerful, for instance, without also being your best self will only lead to loneliness and disappointment.

Whatever you do in life, no matter how special that is, if you aren't also loving, kind, courageous, strong, honest, and true to your true nature, you will not be happy. And the opposite is true: Whatever you do in life, no matter how lowly, if you are also loving, kind, courageous, strong, honest, and true to your true nature, you will be happy, and at the end of your life, you'll be satisfied with that life. That is the measure of a "successful" life: Have I been true to my true nature as love?

It is *how you are* in life, not what you do in life that will make you and your soul happy. And yet, being your best self is not easy. Every minute of your life, you are challenged by something called the ego, which is the programming you've been given that keeps you from being your best self, from being the divine being that you actually are. The ego is the weight you're lifting to get stronger in love. It's the reason effort is needed to be loving.

People live hundreds, if not thousands, of lifetimes doing the ego's bidding and discovering the emptiness of this before they begin to see the truth about what really matters: Love is all that matters. Without love, your life will feel meaningless, no matter what you do. Why? Because you are to discover the power and importance of love and further develop it, and this is done by spending lifetime after lifetime going after what doesn't make you truly happy, by going after what the ego wants while ignoring what's more important to one's happiness: love.

At some point in your evolution, you finally get it: Love is what matters. However, that's only the beginning, because now you have to learn to overcome the ego, the programming that goes against love, and that will take many, many more lifetimes.

I know this sounds like a long time, because a lifetime feels like a very long time to you as a human being. But to the soul, each lifetime is like a blink of an eye or a dream you had: While you were dreaming, you were engrossed in what seemed to be a very long adventure, but in reality, that adventure took only a few minutes.

You are living in a dream of sorts, where time feels the way it does, but where time, in fact, has no reality. This is something that can't be grasped by you while you're living inside this "dream," since the illusion of being a human being with an ego and all its desires and fears seems so very real and so very difficult. But, although it *is* difficult and we have compassion for that, your human life is not as real as you think, and like a dream, one day you will "wake up" from it and find yourself back in your comfortable, safe bed, none the worse for it.

This awakening from the dream is called death by those in the dream, but it is actually a continuation of life from a different, freer perspective. You are still yourself, in a sense, but without all the pain and negative emotions you felt as a human being. You still remember what it was like to be human, but you experience yourself as much freer and lighter, and you're eager to return to the challenges of human existence.

This sounds like a fairytale, and the human experience is like a fairytale to some extent: The hero or heroine faces the challenge of the evil queen or dragon and overcomes this challenge with love of all that is good and with right action, courage, perseverance, patience, hope, and fortitude.

You are told these stories as children because such tales of love and courage are embedded in your DNA as the way out of the horror you find yourselves in. Your soul has chosen a difficult challenge *and* it has the inner strength to overcome the dragon of the ego. You are given both the challenge and the inner strength to overcome the challenge. Much more is said about this in a previous book of mine called *A Heroic Life*.

You came from God, and you will return to God, but it is a very long journey. God sends out aspects of itself—souls—to explore creation and to further create. What a marvelous existence this is! You exist as God *and* as God's creations. But since God lives within you, you are more like God's hands and feet and eyes and ears. You are both an explorer and a creator—and what could be more fun!

You are more than "made in God's image;" you *are* God, an aspect or spun off spark of God, one that is continually in touch with the whole of God. You and all of creation are divine! However, there are places within creation in which God chooses to become lost for a while to experience what that would be like. Earth is one of those places. God has created programming, stored in your DNA, that allows God to have not only a unique experience of life on this planet as a particular character, but also an experience of being divorced from Source and to some extent divorced from love, made possible by programming that is the ego.

The human experience on planet Earth is one of the more challenging experiences that God is having, which is what makes it so powerful—powerfully transformative and enriching to God. The greater the challenge, the greater the potential for growth and the soul's evolution. I'm sure you can relate to this: The most difficult experiences you've had in life, no doubt, have had the greatest impact on you and transformed you the most. Now, while it is true that not everyone learns and grows from an experience as their soul intends, the *potential* is always there for transformation, or at least eventual transformation, and for learning things that couldn't have been learned any other way.

Compassion, for example, is one of those things that can only be learned by having certain experiences—by "walking in another's shoes." As a result, many of your lifetimes on Earth are exactly that: You have an experience for the purpose of understanding what it feels like to have that experience so that when you meet another who's had that experience, you'll understand its impact and have compassion for what that person went through. That compassion is the beginning of love. Compassion opens you to another.

Love is impossible without a compassionate heart, which takes time—lifetimes—to develop. A lack of compassion leads to hurting others, while compassion makes it difficult to hurt others—to do "unto others" what you would *not* want "done unto" you. The Golden rule is golden because it is a reliable measure for behavior based on love: Do unto others as you would have them do unto you; and conversely: don't do unto others what you don't want done unto you.

Sometimes, you'll have to experience something being "done unto you" to understand why that should not be done. In your earliest lifetimes, many of your lessons are of this nature: The negative consequences of your actions dissuade you from repeating that behavior. Those consequences come in many forms: incarceration, having to pay restitution, losing love and respect from others, being shunned, being hurt or murdered or retaliated against in some other way, to name a few. This is how love is learned: You act unlovingly and reap the painful results of that. Then, when you consider doing that again, you're more likely to make a better choice.

This is elementary: You do unto others as you would have them do unto you because doing anything other than this will ultimately be harmful to you, not only to others. It will cause you to suffer, if not immediately, then down the road, and if not in this lifetime, then in another, as karma delivers the needed lesson of love.

You have been given a moral compass that steers you toward love, but you must pay attention to this compass, or it is no good. This compass steers you by way of suffering: When you do something that goes against love, you feel bad, you make others feel bad, and you may experience other negative consequences as well. Even if society or others don't punish you in some way, when you don't follow your moral compass, you'll still experience an immediate and unpleasant contraction of your state of consciousness, a negative state.

I grant you that there is a small percentage of people who do not seem to have a moral compass or who persist in not following it, but even they do have a moral compass. No one is without one. It is one of the ways that God makes sure to remember that He/She chose to get lost in being a human being for a while. In this way, suffering is a gift. It is part of life and must be part of life, or God might become so divorced from love as to not find His/Her way back to love.

Another system was created to ensure that God doesn't permanently get caught in creation and in forgetfulness of His/Her inherent divinity: helpers from other dimensions and even within the third dimension who remind you of who you really are and point you back to love. Karma and your moral compass are not the only things keeping you on track and steering you back Home. You are given helpers, both in the body on Earth and out of the body on higher dimensions, who provide the messages, encouragement, insights, and other things you need to evolve and progress toward love.

These helpers come in various forms: enlightened beings who incarnate to teach and uplift humanity, such as myself in my lifetime as Jesus; angels, who have never incarnated in third dimension; and guides and Ascended Masters, who mastered the third dimension and who choose to be involved in serving this dimension. These are the ones I will be focusing on here.

There have also been others involved with you, such as Pleiadians and other extraterrestrial races, many of whom are related to humanity in some way and love you deeply, as well as more unhelpful elements who meddle in human affairs from time to time.

The Creator has created a hierarchy of sorts to care for and foster itself as the Creator evolves through creation, but it is a hierarchy based on service, not on power, as the beings who are farther along in their spiritual evolution serve only out of love and no other motive. What they receive in exchange for their service is the joy of loving and serving creation in addition to the furtherance of their soul's evolution. So, that is the design: Those farther along in their evolution help those less far along. That way, everyone is learning and evolving and everyone is gaining in love.

This is true of human beings as well: Those with more wisdom and spiritual advancement invariably serve those with less wisdom. And those who are more spiritually advanced raise the consciousnesses of those who are less advanced by transmitting a higher state of consciousness, as do we on other dimensions.

To return to the topic of this chapter, as I said, you came from God, and you will return to God. This returning is the ultimate reunion, but it is by no means an end to life, only a completion of your soul's mission to enrich the godhead. After your soul has completed its journey, a merging happens that is more like a joining than a dissolving: You become God in a way that is different than before your soul embarked on this journey. Words are inadequate to express or explain this any further.

When your soul spun off from the godhead, it was the same as God, in the same way that a spark of fire is still fire but separate from the flame it came from. Your essence has always been of God, but your soul separated from God in order to have its own unique experiences, which enrich the godhead as much as they enrich your own soul. Everything you experience and learn also expands the Creator in understanding and love. And you are never actually separate from God. In this way, the analogy of the spark doesn't hold, for you are, paradoxically, both apart from God but not apart from God, since you are connected through your essence and still able to know God intimately, as God abides within you throughout your journey.

However, in order to have certain experiences, your soul needs to separate even further at times, although not every soul chooses to do this. Angels, for instance, do not choose to separate further in this way but to remain close to the godhead. If they do choose to separate further at a certain point, they become what you call "fallen angels," meaning they'll no longer be able to return to being angels. Most angels eventually do choose to separate further out of pure curiosity and also out of a desire to evolve and serve in a different way. As you can imagine, making this choice is a momentous turning point in a soul's evolution.

Once a soul is spun off from the godhead, it's free to make any number of choices, all of which lead to various unique experiences, which is the purpose of leaving the godhead. All choices are acceptable and honored. Free will is not only a feature of human life in the third dimension, but also of sentient life in general, including animals and plants, who do sense and move on their own accord and have a certain awareness of their existence, which is what I mean by "sentient" here.

Life in its various forms has programming that sets the stage for a particular kind of life, and it has free will. The strength and degree of a lifeform's programming can make it seem like they don't have free will, but even plants have some degree of free will, and you know from experiences with your pets that they have distinct personalities and do make choices that aren't part of their programming.

Free will is an important feature of the divine plan. Without the ability to program creations and give them free will, the Divine couldn't have the experiences it has. Programming makes you unique and blocks the awareness of where you came from and who you really are, and free will allows for choices to be made that the Divine would never make. Without programming, the Divine would only choose love and experience love; and with programming and free will, the Divine can make and explore an infinite number of choices. The possibilities are truly endless, and all are rich and enriching to the Creator.

To understand why the Creator would do this, you have to tap in to the part of you that loves a challenge and loves to be surprised and the part of you that loves to have experiences, grow, and learn. This is your divine self, your true nature. It loves exploration, growth, change, variety, and all kinds of experiences because it's curious and interested in life's possibilities.

You actually love this crazy rollercoaster ride you're on! Can you experience that love for adventure and for the unknown within you? This love for adventure and experience is why you love movies and books. What you love about them is that you're able to experience things you've never and will never experience. Through movies and books, you get to vicariously experience all sorts of situations, characters, and possibilities in the comfort and safety of your home.

That's a little like what the Divine experiences through you as you have your various experiences. The Divine is untouched, unharmed by any experience, only expanded. And the truth is that your soul, your divine nature, is also untouched and unharmed by the experiences you have. Your character goes through them, but you are not this character. And like an actor at the end of a play, at the end of your life, you take off your costume and makeup and declare that it was a good show!

This may sound callous, but that's only because seeing life from your soul's perspective is difficult. But when this life is over, you'll be able to see your life and that of others from a much broader and truer perspective, from your soul's perspective. Then, you'll rejoice in the opportunity this life has afforded you to have the experiences you've had to learn, grow, love, and create. You are not who you *think* you are!

Programming and free will allow you to have a unique and interesting experience, one unlike anyone else has ever or will ever have. No one is exactly like you, no time or place or culture is exactly like the time and place and culture you live in, and no experience you have is exactly like anyone else's experience.

This uniqueness deserves to be celebrated, as the Divine celebrates it. To long to be like or look like someone else or have the life someone else is having is not only impossible, but a waste of your precious energy. Such longings come from the ego (i.e., your programming), and they steal your joy and potential for loving yourself and others. All of your thoughts of comparison and all of your desires and judgments in relation to others are useless and only take you away from living the fullest life possible as the character you came here to be. Love yourself just as you are and for your uniqueness. You are incomparable. This is one of the most important lessons of love.

You can live your best life, but it will be as this character, not some other character you might prefer. What do you think your soul intended in making the choices it did, in designing this character as it did, in giving what it gave you and not giving you what it didn't give you?

Your circumstances were designed by your soul for you with a specific intention, and your job is to align with that intention and to live the life your soul intended. The purpose of this book is to help you do that. The only reason learning about angels, Ascended Masters, and guides is important is that this understanding might help you align with the help you're being given from other dimensions to live your best life, which is our wish for you.

Chapter 2
Working with Angels

What Angels Do and How to Work with Them

Much about angels has already been written by others, but I will weigh in on this subject by providing what I think will be most helpful to you in healing and progressing spiritually. Healing is a particular expertise of angels, who are not only messengers, as they are commonly called, but healers. Angels are like the white blood cells in your own body, which combat infection and respond to illness, and also like red blood cells, which deliver gases and nutrients throughout the body. Without angels, God's body, if you will, wouldn't function properly. The Divine needs angels to accomplish what it wants to do within creation. Angels are essential components of all life, not just on the material plane, or third dimension, but throughout the dimensions.

Angels are of a higher order and don't usually have a relationship with specific individuals over a long period of time, as spirit guides do. Rather, they come and go as needed throughout the body of God. Angels go where they are called and where they feel called, and when that mission is complete, they go on to another mission, often in an entirely different dimension or star system. They operate in all dimensions and, at times, interact with human beings to deliver messages and healing. However, their interactions with humans are but a small part of what they do.

This is quite different from spirit guides and Ascended Masters, who are particularly devoted to Earth and other third dimensional societies. Guides and Ascended Masters are engaged in long-term undertakings with human beings and involved more closely with specific individuals than angels. The work of guides and Ascended Masters is focused most on those, like yourselves, who are reincarnating in third dimension and also, to some extent, on those in the fourth dimension, or the astral plane, which is where you go in between lifetimes. The fourth dimension is where angels are more closely involved with humans, as they, along with your spirit guides, help people transition from the third to the fourth dimension at death and then back again to the third dimension at birth.

Anyone can call on angels for help, and either they or another who they summon on their behalf will answer your call. In this way, angels are very available to humanity, but often they will simply assemble appropriate guides and other helpers to assist you in what you are praying for rather than answer your call themselves. This is one of the ways they are messengers: They deliver your requests for help to the appropriate and best helpers for you and your situation.

You often hear of guardian angels being by your side, protecting and guiding you, and while it's true that each of you has numerous spirit guides who protect and guide you moment to moment, guiding you day-to-day is not specifically an angel's job. Angels are not the ones best suited to guiding your human life, since they've never been human, while your guides and the Ascended Masters have graduated from the third dimension and personally understand what it's like to be human and to overcome the human ego. It's understandable that spirit guides have often been mistakenly called "angels" or "guardian angels" and that's fine. I point this out only to bring a little more clarity to this subject.

Just as red blood cells circulate throughout your body, angels circulate throughout the dimensions, transmitting needed information from one place to another. They are the Divine's communication system. Angels are able to see what needs to be done throughout the dimensions and coordinate the actions that need to be taken.

Because angels are so essential to the health and maintenance of the body of the Divine, there will always be souls spun off from the godhead who will play this role, at least for a time. Just as your body produces red blood cells as needed, the Divine produces souls that become angels as needed.

It's impossible for you to understand what it's like to be an angel, and it also isn't necessary. Angels are so very different from human beings, although not so different from your true nature. Still, what you experience of your true nature is so significantly limited and colored by the experience of having a body-mind that even people who are enlightened can't fully know the nature of angels or of the Divine. However, once you leave the body and exist in higher dimensions, your experience of God expands to include a truer sense of this. But not until then will you have a better sense of the enormity and magnificence of God.

For the time being, you are in a human body and limited by that experience. Nevertheless, you are still able to receive communications from your soul through your spirit guides and others via your intuition to ease your suffering and help you evolve. Your guides send you insights intuitively, encourage you to move in certain directions and not others, send people to help you, put information you need in front you, arrange circumstances for your growth, and motivate others to help you and provide certain opportunities.

Every minute of your life, your guides are involved with you in one way or another. They are always looking out for you and have your best interests at heart. Your guides know you intimately because most of them have been with you for lifetimes, and some have been with you for eons. Your guides are dedicated to you and to your growth almost exclusively. This is how much each and every one of you is loved. Each of you is given what you need in every moment of your life. Your guides are that close and that available to you.

Angels have a different relationship to human beings, if you could even call it that, since most people's relationship with any particular angel is likely to be brief and infrequent. However, some psychics and channels have a more regular, ongoing relationship with one or more angels because of the nature of their work.

Many angels do deliver information through channels and also work through healers, particularly energy workers, as channeling healing energy to humanity is one way that angels do serve people who are open to them. Healers who have some psychic awareness often see or feel angels around them when they're working and may also receive messages related to healing from angels.

Angels usually choose to appear to psychics, healers, and others in a form that can be recognized as an angel, since everyone grows up with certain ideas about what angels look like. In truth, angels don't have wings or any physicality at all. They don't look the way people assume they look, but angels will take on that guise to play the role and to demonstrate that they're angels.

An angel's true appearance is that of pure energy, but when interacting with people, taking on a more personified appearance, one human beings can relate to, usually serves the relationship. This reinforces what people believe angels look like, so angels continue to appear to people that way, and people continue to assume that's how angels look.

Originally, when artists depicted wings on angels, they were undoubtedly trying to convey their swift appearance and disappearance and their nature as messengers who fly from place to place. However, the truth is, if you were able to see angels as they actually are, they would appear as a brilliant light, although you would be seeing only a mere pinpoint of their entire energy, as their brilliance is too much to behold. Angels have to tamp down their energy when they interact with people, or their energy would be impossible for people to bear.

In addition to being messengers for the Divine, like white blood cells in your own body, angels fend off what might corrupt or harm the body of God and bring healing to where healing is needed. Because you have free will and because duality is present throughout creation, meaning there is both love and an absence of love within creation, a positive pole and a negative pole, at times a rebalancing of the system is needed, which is accomplished, in part, through healing those who have lost their way.

God doesn't allow Himself/Herself to get so lost in the negative pole that returning to Love is impossible. Angels are the mechanism that rebalances duality and brings individuals back into the fold. Like the parable of the good shepherd who won't allow even one sheep to be lost to love, angels are sent out to summon those who've fallen into Darkness back into the Light.

The process of rescuing a lost soul can take quite a while because every being is free to refuse to go toward Love, but eventually, everyone does choose this under the patient and gentle persuasion of the angels.

Those who are used to "living by the sword" as opposed to love view love as weak and power and hatred as strong. They've come to believe that love doesn't actually exist and is, therefore, a useless concept. That's how far they've fallen away from love. They don't know the rewards of love and don't believe in love.

How do you get them to believe in love again? This is often a slow and somewhat painful process, because it's painful and humbling to see that you've been wrong. But the rewards are great. To discover that the beliefs you've held that have caused you so much pain are false and that there's a better, happier way to live is really good news!

Some of those who've fallen into such darkness are nonphysical beings who have never had human lifetimes, and the route to healing for many of them is to enter a cycle of reincarnation on Earth or elsewhere, where they'll learn about love. But first, their soul will have to undergo some healing before it will be ready to take on such a challenge as earthly lifetimes.

Angels take these individuals to a hospital of sorts where they receive whatever they need to recover from their mistaken beliefs and from the wounds they've inflicted on themselves and others. Then, when they're ready, they'll reincarnate into circumstances that will foster love.

This is the same type of care that human beings who've led a hateful or violent life receive after they die. No one who has led a painful or destructive lifetime is sent into another lifetime without adequate healing in between lives to ensure that their errors aren't repeated. Individuals are always given what they need to be able to have a better, happier, and more loving life next time around, and this is usually what happens. Much progress is made in between lifetimes, and angels play an important role in this healing.

Angels may not understand what it's like to be human, but they do know God, and that's what angels bring to those who need healing: They bring the presence of God. They infuse those they care for with the Love and Light of the Creator. This is how they heal, not with words but with a transmission of Love.

Angels are powerful light beings who share their Love and Light with whomever they encounter. This is why they are present at births, deaths, and other important transitions and events, since it is during such times that the Love and Light of the Creator is most needed. Angels are also present during extreme, life-threatening situations, such as accidents, cataclysms, and on the battlefield, to shape the outcome. They're there to help those who are meant to transition to the afterlife and to save those who aren't meant to die.

There have been many accounts from survivors who saw angels or felt their presence or had the experience of being lifted out of harm's way by them. These were not imaginations but real occurrences. Miracles do happen, and under extreme circumstances, angels may intervene and perform what you would call a miracle.

During such times, some people get a glimpse of the beings who reside in other dimensions, who don't otherwise allow themselves to be seen because this would be too disruptive to your human life. But sometimes miracles serve and sometimes miracles are necessary.

Angels frequently allow themselves to be seen by those dying because such visions help prepare the dying for the afterlife. Helping people cross over is one of their jobs, as angels, and it is an important one. Angels appear to those dying to comfort them, bring them peace, help them come to grips with their death and the life they've lived, and deliver messages of love and hope. They show the dying images of what awaits them and images of their loved ones waiting for them. And sometimes, their loved ones also appear and speak encouragingly to them. The message that angels deliver to the dying is simply: "All is well. It's your time to go, and you're going to a beautiful place where you're loved and where you'll be greeted by your loved ones." And this is true.

Once death has taken place, an angel's job is rarely over, for they, along with your guides and others, are often involved in healing in the afterlife, as healing is almost always necessary as part of adjusting to the afterlife. The former life needs to be examined and processed and misunderstandings healed in what many have called the "life review." This is accomplished, in part, by showing those who have died truths about themselves and others and about that lifetime that they weren't able to see while they were alive.

Angels are frequently at the life review because of their importance in providing healing and help as the individual becomes accustomed to the afterlife. Angels assist with both the death and the adjustment period following death, where healing takes place and misunderstandings are set right. When an individual is ready to move on from this period of healing, the angels' work is complete.

The healing role that angels play is to channel God's energy—the energy of pure Love. This unconditional love heals on deep, deep levels, beyond all intellectual understanding or insight. Guides bring healing through understanding and insight, while angels bring healing through the energy of Love.

This Love is unlike anything you have ever experienced in life. It is of another magnitude. The love you experience as a human is a watered-down version of the unconditional love of the godhead. Nevertheless, you've experienced this Love many, many times—every time you've been in between lifetimes—and on some level, you remember this Love and know the truth of what I am saying. This is the angels' job: To bring you closer to God and to your true nature as Love by giving you a taste of this Love, an *experience* of this Love. And that, alone, is healing.

Angels can be summoned for healing by anyone who needs it, by those who work as healers, and by anyone on behalf of others. Angels are glad to answer your call and will assemble others who can be especially helpful in ways that they, themselves, may not be able to be. They, along with your guides, will also arrange circumstances in your life conducive to your healing. For instance, they may send someone your way who has the insight or information you need for the next step in your healing journey.

Healing is a journey, and it does take time, so patience is needed. Calling on angels and guides for healing is the first step. It sets in motion any number of events that will lead to healing or accelerate the healing that is already taking place; however, much more is involved in healing than just praying for it.

Once you've prayed for healing, there are things you need to do to cooperate with and support that healing. Your spiritual and emotional growth, which is behind the need for most healing, requires effort and commitment on your part to putting into action the inspirations and intuitions you receive from your spirit guides. Your healing journey is designed and led by your guides through your intuition, but you must follow that intuitive guidance and take the necessary steps on that journey.

For instance, you may be intuitively guided to work with a particular healer or a number of healers to clear the emotional debris that blocks your spiritual growth. The need for emotional healing is what most impedes spiritual seekers on the path and, in general, prevents people from living their best life. It's a rare individual who doesn't need some help in overcoming the limitations and blocks imposed by early childhood conditioning.

Even the best parents are imperfect human beings, and children draw mistaken conclusions about themselves even under the best of circumstances. To assume that you don't need healing is probably your ego's wishful thinking and not the truth. There will come a time, when humanity is more evolved, when there will be far less need for emotional healing and far better methods than there are now, but that's a distant dream. Your current methods are primitive at best; and yet, they're better than nothing.

One of the greatest tools you have for healing is prayer, for not only does it summon nonphysical forces to your side, but it can open you up to a relationship with God that is, in itself, healing. So much of the wounding in early childhood happens as a result of unhappy and sometimes even abusive parents. Feelings towards one's parents get displaced onto God, and God becomes The Punisher or The Withholder or The Uncaring One.

An inadequate relationship with one's parents affects a person's entire outlook on life and on God. How can you feel good about life and about God when your early experiences of life and your god-like parents were hurtful? Children who receive inadequate or harsh parenting come to negative conclusions about themselves, others, life, and God that, unless examined, affect every aspect of their lives and their capacity for happiness. Healing is necessary and important to becoming a happy and healthy human being and to having a happy and healthy society.

Prayer can heal your relationship to God, but you have to be willing to open the door on your end to having a relationship. Please dismiss any childhood notions you might have about God. God is not an entity or a person and certainly not judgmental and punishing, as some religions have described. When I speak of God, I'm speaking of the force behind all creation, which is powered by love, not the personal love you know, but something you can't experience fully while you are in a human body.

God is everything you consider good and admirable about human beings magnified beyond measure and so much more. God is beauty, God is creativity, God is peace, God is supreme wisdom and intelligence, God is the lifeforce that streams through every creation in the unimaginably infinite body of God. God is goodness, God is love, and this is the truth. To know this at your core is to be healed because, then, you can't help but also know *yourself* as love, and when you know yourself as love, you are healed.

To have a relationship with God is to feel connected to something greater than yourself that is pure goodness and has your best interests at heart. Opening to such a relationship is a way of saying: "I trust life to be good and to bring me whatever is in my highest good, and I want to align with that and with all that is good." This is one of the first and most important steps in the healing process.

Your guides and the Ascended Masters are emissaries, or intermediaries, for God, so knowing about them and addressing them in prayer is another, perhaps more relatable, way of connecting with God and the love and beneficence of creation.

Trust in the goodness of life is essential for a happy and fulfilling life, since not trusting that life is good is a self-fulfilling prophecy: That belief creates the experience that life is *not* good because it causes you to contract into your egoic self and take your cues from the ego, and the life the ego creates will not be your best life.

This is the problem with a challenging childhood: It makes it difficult to trust life, yourself, and others. This distrust is a low-grade state of fear, which keeps you in your primitive, lower brain and in the grip of the ego, which is problematic in so many ways.

Listening to the ego, which speaks to you through the voice in your head, is the cause of all suffering and all of the conflict and violence in the world—and the cause of self-hatred. Listening to this voice, which you think of as your own thoughts, causes both missteps and wars. This is because the ego isn't wise. It doesn't know what your best life looks like. It isn't privy to your soul's plan and, therefore, not capable of guiding you. Listening to the voice in your head is like getting advice from Siri or Alexa (i.e., a computer-generated voice) for how to live your life. Is it any wonder most people don't love themselves, when they believe that this petty and self-possessed voice in their head is true and represents who they are?

So, how do you get from distrust to trusting life, from negativity to positivity? The answer to that is basically the description of the healing journey, and it's different for every person. However, one thing people on this journey have in common: They're willing to discover things about themselves that they didn't know. They're willing to learn and grow. Once you demonstrate this readiness and willingness to grow, your soul will bring you what you need to grow. It will put teachers, healers, helpers, books, seminars, retreats, opportunities, and information in front of you, and your job is to say yes to what you feel drawn to and follow through on that yes.

Knowing what to say yes to and what not to is not as difficult as it may seem, because you actually know what's true for you to do. You know this because you feel excited, curious, and energized—you feel a yes and a sense of joy—when you encounter what fits for you or when you think about it. And the converse is also true: You feel a no, a lack of energy and joy, around possibilities that are not for you.

These are the ways your soul and your guides communicate with you, which everyone is familiar with. But honoring these intuitions and nudges is another story, because the egoic mind, or the voice in your head, will list reasons for *not* doing something, no matter what that is.

The rational mind's job is to reason—to make lists of pros and cons, for example, which is very useful at times—and the egoic mind's job is to make decisions. Where do these decisions come from? What's the basis for making a decision? Usually, the egoic mind weighs things according to its values: Will it be expensive? Will it be safe? Will it be a lot of effort? Will it be comfortable? Will it make me richer or more popular? What will other people think? The egoic mind decides whether or not to do something based on convenience, comfort, ease, and "what's in it for me."

These are not good guidelines for those interested in growth, which isn't convenient, comfortable, or easy and often involves a significant commitment of money, effort, and time. The ego doesn't value growth, so activities that foster growth, are not high on the ego's to-do list, if they're on there at all.

If you're interested in growing, you're interested in this because your soul and your true self love growing and want to grow *despite* the ego's objections. The spiritual path is all about overcoming the ego, and one of the most important things you can do toward that end is emotional healing work, which the ego will resist at every turn, and it will give you lots of good reasons, from its standpoint, for resisting growth. No, the voice in your head won't be useful on the spiritual path. It will keep you from living your best life, and it has always been what has kept you from living your best life.

More will be said about healing throughout this book. For now, I'd like to explain how angels can help you heal your emotional wounds and issues. First of all, you have to call on angels for their help, as they need to be called in. Your guides are always available to help you through anything you're experiencing, and angels count on your guides to do that work unless your guides or you invite them to also help.

What guides will call angels in to do and what you can call them in to do is to clear negative energies and entities. So, let me explain what I mean by "negative energies and entities." Negative energies are easy enough to explain. If people are in a negative state for a while, negative thoughtforms accumulate around them, which create a negative field of energy, a negative vibrational state. Unless dissipated by positive thoughts, negative thoughtforms will collect and strengthen. The same happens with positive thoughts: They accumulate around someone, forming a shield against negative energies.

A person's vibration is the sum total of the positive and negative thoughts that have accumulated around a person at a particular time. Your vibration is not static but ever-changing according to the ideas you're entertaining. So, even a generally positive person can get taken over by negativity if he or she dwells on negative thoughts for an extended time. Getting into a positive state is, in part, a matter of entertaining positive ideas, or at least *not* entertaining negative ones, while getting into a negative state is a matter of dwelling on negative ideas.

The ideas you input from others and from the media also affect your vibrational state. Taking in a lot of negative ideas and feelings from others or from the media will lower your vibration, even though they aren't *your* thoughts and feelings. In this way, *your* vibration isn't entirely yours but affected by everything and everyone around you.

This is why it is so important—if you're interested in healing yourselves, healing others, or healing the planet—to keep your vibration high, or to be positive, as much as possible. Your vibration is broadcasted to others, who are affected by it. Many of you are healing and uplifting others without even knowing it because you broadcast a higher vibration than most, and the opposite is true: Some people are quite toxic to others, who feel that negativity and respond by either avoiding them or joining them in their misery. Life doesn't go well for those broadcasting negativity, who often feel victimized by life. But their own negative thoughts and feelings are what is victimizing them.

Fortunately, this can be remedied, and I will say more about this in the next chapter. However, some people fall so far down the rabbit hole of negativity that they can't pull themselves out and continually hurt themselves and others with further negativity. When this is the case, certain drugs may be helpful in turning this vicious cycle around and helping them regain a more positive perspective, along with other interventions.

When negativity has progressed this far, usually negative nonphysical beings are involved. When you're vibrating at a certain lower frequency, you draw to you nonphysical beings who also vibrate at that lower frequency, who "hang out" with you and are able to influence you.

Some of these nonphysical beings are human beings who have died who are seeking to be involved with humans inappropriately to fulfill some need, such as an addiction, or who want revenge or simply to trick and manipulate people for fun or to feel powerful, which may have been something they also did when they were alive.

However, there are nonphysical beings that are more problematic and common than disembodied humans that belong to a class of nonphysical beings I will call "negative entities" or "entities" for short, who have never been human and who have lost their way and no longer believe in love. They exist on the astral plane with others of their vibration who also don't believe in love, so this belief is reinforced and seems very real and true to them.

The life of these negative entities consists of trying to gain status and power amongst themselves, which they attain by bringing human beings down to their lower vibration. Theirs is a hierarchy built on gaining power through causing pain to human beings, with the ultimate goal of getting them to commit suicide. That is how these entities believe they will escape some of the pain they're experiencing.

Fear is what keeps entities doing what they do. They are afraid of other entities who have more power. More powerful entities have lied to them about the nature of the universe. These more powerful entities don't realize they are lying; they're just passing on what they've been told. All entities believe that the Light is a place of dissolution of all will and therefore power. They can't imagine happiness, love, or peace because they don't experience them, so the promise of these is empty.

Because of these lies, entities are afraid of angels, which is why entities do listen to angels when angels tell them to stop what they're doing. Some entities, mostly ones with little power, decide that going into the Light can't possibly be worse than their current plight, and they go with the angels and are pleasantly surprised. Many of the beings of light who work with angels to clear negative entities were once lost souls themselves.

Negative entities are able to cause people a great deal of pain by magnifying any negativity that's already there. Your own egoic minds are, by nature, negative and fearful, and when you fall prey to your egoic thoughts and stay in that negativity long enough to lower your vibration significantly, entities are able to plant thoughts into your mind.

I'm sure that those of you who've experienced a deep depression or persistent sadness, guilt, anger, or other strong negative emotions can relate to this. When your thoughts become particularly dark, hopeless, violent, or suicidal, you can be sure negative entities are responsible. People you consider evil, for instance, such as murderers and rapists, are under the spell of such entities, or they wouldn't be able to carry out such acts. This is what happens when entities and human beings become so divorced from love that they no longer feel love or believe in it.

Angels are the ones who remove entities from humans and send them into the Light. Then, angels pour the Love and Light of the Creator into the places in your energy field that need it, to mend the wound that allowed the entity or entities to attach in the first place. People's energy fields have places of congealed energy that represent emotional complexes as well as tears, or holes, that allow entities to attach. Angels untangle the complexes, remove the entities, and fill the holes with Light.

Angels know exactly how to do this. All you have to do is call on them, and they do the repair work energetically. Although your energy field will eventually return to its previous shape if your thoughts and emotions don't change, this repair work can afford enough temporary relief from negative patterns to make it more possible to change your relationship to your thoughts.

It isn't difficult for angels to remove entities when asked, but you have to ask. That's why it's important for you to know about entities and what to do about them. I'm telling you about them so that you can take steps to rid yourself of them. It isn't good for you or for them to be around you. There is no need to be afraid of entities. All they have ever been able to do is plant negative thoughts into your mind. Knowing about them will empower you to send them away and stop being affected by such thoughts.

Clearing Entities

The good news is that the biggest hurdle to getting rid of entities is not knowing they exist. In most cases, entities are not difficult to get rid of, and nearly anyone can clear them. In fact, it's a good idea to clear them periodically, since they tend to come back during challenging and stressful times. Whenever ego-identification and emotions are strong, entity attachment can recur. Entity attachment can happen even to those who are very advanced spiritually. They remain vulnerable to entities because ego-identification can still happen, and when it does, entities are more than happy to try to keep that identification and those negative feelings going.

What's most important for you to understand is that entities are not powerful, not in your realm or in any other. The only power they have is what you give them by believing the thoughts they plant in your mind or by being afraid of them because you believe that they are powerful. Entities feed on negative feelings, especially fear, meaning they grow in confidence and brazenness when fear and other negative feelings are present.

Given this, being fearful in general or being afraid of them will only draw them to you or keep them there. Fear and other negative emotions allow entities to influence your consciousness, while love and other positive emotions drain entities of confidence and repel them. The good news is that there is truly "nothing to fear but fear itself," as fears are simply imaginations of something negative in the future, not anything real in the here and now.

If you are doing a clearing by yourself, you need to be free from fear and negativity and in a positive state of mind to be successful in dispelling the entities. You need to feel confident, safe, protected, and aligned with all that is good. Calling on angels and guides to protect you and help you align with all that is good is a good way to begin any clearing. Even if you aren't able to remain positive, entities can't harm you in any way other than the ways they have. But they may not be convinced to leave if you, yourself, aren't able to believe in the power of love and express a commitment to it.

Being positive can be a challenge. If you've been living with a lot of negativity, you may not feel love or the presence of loving spiritual forces. You may have taken on the entities' point of view to the extent that it makes it difficult to feel positive feelings and align with a more positive viewpoint about yourself and life. If that's the case, it may be necessary to work with a healer who is used to doing this kind of work and who can help you get to the bottom of some of the negative beliefs that have allowed any entities to be there.

Healers who are intuitive or psychic and who can receive information from the angels and your guides are best able to do this work. This is most often the work of shamans and those who call themselves energy healers or energy workers. Once you do this work with a healer, perhaps a few times, it will be more possible to do it on your own.

Here's how to proceed with a clearing: Once you've quieted your mind and moved into a peaceful, positive emotional space, call in the angels and ask for their protection and assistance in clearing any negative entities and affirm your willingness and readiness to receive their insight and healing. Your prayer can be something like this:

> *"I call on angels to release me from any negative entities that might be keeping me from being the loving and best human being I can be. I am ready and willing to have any entities removed now, and I will do my best to heal and raise my vibration so that they can't return. Also, please give me insight into the negative beliefs that allowed these entities to attach and help me heal those issues. Thank you for your help."*

After this initial clearing, you may need to do other clearings regularly, at least for a while, to reinforce and maintain the healing and prevent the entities from returning. The specific words you use during this clearing aren't important. Your intent is what is responded to by both the angels and the entities. The intent to clear the entities sets the process in motion and brings about whatever needs to happen.

For this process to be successful over time, it's important to maintain positive thoughts and feelings as much as possible every day. This will strengthen your ability to stave off intruders and establish a new, more positive way of thinking. Throughout your day, whenever you find yourself caught in negative thoughts or feelings, ask angels for assistance in clearing that negativity. Also ask for assistance in uncovering any beliefs that underlie the negative feelings. Take time to be quiet and listen for answers to what beliefs caused the negative feelings. What did you say to yourself that made you feel that way? More will be said about how to do this and other healing work in the next chapter.

Chapter 3
Freeing Yourself from Negative Emotions

Feelings arise and sometimes take you over, so then, what do you do? When you're feeling angry, afraid, sad, or upset in some way, that's an opportunity to do some inquiry to discover the mistaken beliefs behind your feelings. There's a way of dealing with feelings that is neither repressing them nor expressing them, which is usually destructive, and that is to *be with* them: Allow any feelings to be there, and be with the sensations and the *experience* of those feelings in your body with acceptance and curiosity. Much of what follows is taken from an earlier book by this author called *Getting Free: Moving Beyond Negativity and Limiting Beliefs*.

Being with Difficult Feelings

Whenever you're experiencing an unpleasant emotion, such as anger or fear, just notice that you are feeling that. Then, take a few deep breaths and choose to stop thinking whatever you are thinking (because that's what got you into trouble in the first place). Instead of being involved in your thoughts, turn your attention onto the sensations of breathing and other sensations in your body. Doing this will help you move into a more rational brain state.

Next, notice what those feelings feel like in your body and simply allow those sensations to be there. Then, bring to those feelings the same curiosity and acceptance that a parent would bring to a hurt child to try to uncover the child's pain. Relate to your feelings as your divine self would, with love, gentleness, kindness, acceptance, curiosity, and a nonjudgmental attitude.

Being with a feeling this way opens up a space for doing some inquiry into those feelings. Then ask: "What was I just thinking that caused me to feel this way? Is it true? What else was I thinking? Is it true?" Keep looking for beliefs that are connected to that feeling and keep asking, "Is it true?"

None of your beliefs are ultimately true, although they certainly may seem true or *feel* true to you. However, they are true only from the ego's perspective. They may be a little true or partially true, which is why they seem true, but partial truths aren't much use and are essentially lies. If those thoughts were completely false, seeing that would be much easier. But like all good conmen and liars, the voice in your head mixes some truth in with the lies to fool you.

Recognizing that the thoughts behind your unpleasant emotions are incomplete statements and, therefore, useless lies is how you weaken and ultimately pull the plug on those emotions. Once you start examining your thoughts this way, you'll see why the word "illusion" is often used to describe the world the ego creates and lives in. The ego sees life and the world through a lens that distorts and, therefore, deludes. It lives in an illusory world of its own imagination. *You* live in this mind-made virtual reality until you see the truth about it and stop giving your thoughts so much attention.

Sitting with a feeling this way invites it to reveal the

reasons it's there. This is a time of receptivity, which requires that you not be involved in thinking. Thoughts may come and go, but the answers you are looking for won't come in the form of thoughts.

What you are waiting and listening for are intuitive knowings. Intuitions are often instantly put into words once they do arise, but the intuitive process is not one of thinking about possible beliefs or trying to figure them out. Instead, your mind is quiet so that you can "hear" your intuition tell you the beliefs behind the feelings, and you wait for as long as it takes.

This material arrives as "Ah-has," a download, an insight, or some other nonverbal flash of knowing. Or an image or a memory from your early life or a previous lifetime might pop into your mind that helps you understand why you feel the way you do or why you believe what you do.

Sitting quietly and waiting patiently affirms your commitment to healing and makes it more possible for your intuition to be heard. The desire to understand the beliefs that produced the feelings and the willingness to take the time to listen open you up to receiving answers. A willingness to ask for help and receive it is all that is really needed to get answers.

When you are doing this investigation, expect that there will be a number of beliefs behind any feeling, and don't just settle for one. Keep listening. Uncovering these beliefs is similar to peeling away the layers of an onion: Uncovering one belief allows you to see the next one. Allow the discovery process to continue as long as it needs to until you feel a sense of completion. Then, be willing to repeat this process if the same feelings arise around a similar circumstance. This process will greatly weaken the conditioning and its ability to cause you to react automatically and unconsciously.

Some beliefs that drive behavior negatively are

unconscious. This is especially true of addictions and compulsions. Being with a feeling in the way that was just described can even uncover unconscious beliefs. Bringing awareness to your feelings without acting on them invites unconscious beliefs to come to the surface. By accepting your feelings and listening to them, you create a safe environment for unconscious material to arise, and so it will. This is why unconscious material often surfaces during meditation. You invite healing by relating to your thoughts and feelings in this gentle, accepting way. Being with feelings this way can greatly speed up your evolution and ease your way through life.

When you work with feelings this way, you may also receive a mental picture or simply a knowing about an event in the past that was responsible for the negative conclusions you came to. These images may be repressed memories from this lifetime or another. These images can be helpful in understanding why you came to the conclusions you did, but you don't need to know the details of the event.

It is more helpful to experience the person you were then and to give that person compassion, acceptance, and also forgiveness, if necessary. You bring the divine self's love, acceptance, wisdom, and compassion to the confused person that came to incorrect conclusions in the midst of a traumatic event. And you offer the same to anyone else who was involved in the traumatic event.

This love and acceptance is what heals, more than uncovering the specific details of what happened. It's much more important to understand what you concluded as a result of some event than to understand exactly what happened or even who was involved.

Feelings happen as a result of what you say to yourself, either consciously or unconsciously. By staying with a feeling with an attitude of curiosity and acceptance, the complex of beliefs that triggered the feeling can be uncovered.

Another thing you can do while sitting with the sensations of an emotion is talk to it—dialogue with that emotion. Find out what it has to say. This is similar to inquiry, but dialoguing has a tendency to uncover things that might not be revealed through inquiry. Dialoguing with an emotion often reveals unconscious material because what you're actually dialoguing with is the unconscious mind. Such a dialogue is an invitation to the unconscious mind to reveal things to you.

This process of healing negative emotions can take some time, and the process may need to be repeated many times before the beliefs and feelings begin to let go. Those beliefs have been there for a very long time, so you can't expect them to disappear the instant you first see them, but seeing them repeatedly in this way, with compassion and acceptance, eventually allows them to release their hold on you. You bring your divine self's compassion to them, and this love is healing.

You don't need to understand or even believe in this process for it to work. You just have to give it a chance, and you'll see for yourself that it does work. There is great healing power in acceptance and compassion. That's clear from psychotherapy. That love and acceptance can free you from suffering is also proof that love is the guiding force behind all life.

Replacing Negative Beliefs with Positive Ones

Once you've uncovered each belief, it's helpful to find a statement that will counteract or neutralize it. The best statement isn't always the opposite of the belief or the negation of it. Sometimes, the opposite belief (e.g. "I'm lovable" instead of

"I'm not lovable") is too big a leap for the unconscious mind and, therefore, unbelievable. Other statements may work better.

For example, if the belief is "I'm not lovable," any of the following statements might be effective in neutralizing it because the unconscious mind might see them as believable: "I am loved by God," "I am open to receiving love," "I freely and gladly give love," "I am a child of God," "Love is here now," "Love is always available," "Love fills me and flows through me," "Love is abundant," "Love is everywhere."

Affirming the presence and abundance of love and your willingness to receive it opens you up to love, while "I'm not lovable" closes you off to the love that is available to you. These affirmations about love are the truth, and this truth will set you free. Affirming your divine self's, or soul's, truth instead of the ego's aligns you with your divine self and heals whatever is false within you. Healing conditioning is largely a matter of moving from the ego's false perspective to the divine self's, and you do that by affirming the divine's self's perspective instead of the ego's.

The key, then, is to find what the divine self or your soul would say to you instead of your ego. Believing its perspective instead of the ego's frees you from your conditioning. By neutralizing the complex of beliefs behind your feelings, the feelings diminish and eventually disappear, and then it's easy to see that your conditioning is just thoughts that arise in your mind and then disappear.

Without feelings attached to them, the thoughts don't have as much power to catch you up. They seem less real, less true, and less compelling. Reprogramming your mind with positive thoughts diminishes the power of the negative thoughts, as the positive thoughts become believed more. Eventually, the negative thoughts will stop arising or rarely arise, and the positive thoughts will be your default state.

Here is a helpful exercise for reprogramming negative beliefs:

Make a list of negative beliefs you hold about yourself, life, and others. For each belief, counteract it with a positive statement or statements — something your divine self or soul would say about you, life, or others. Be your own wise healer by responding to your negative beliefs with the kindness, compassion, and wisdom of your divine self. Doing this will help neutralize the negative belief and any feelings attached to it. Repeat this exercise whenever a negative belief arises, especially when there are feelings attached to it.

This process of reprogramming beliefs does take time, especially if the conditioning is very strong and laden with feelings and if there are many related beliefs. So, you take one belief at a time, and when that belief is seen through, you notice what other beliefs remain. What other belief or beliefs are holding the feelings and the behavior related to those feelings in place? Work on whatever beliefs you are aware of, and eventually the issue will clear.

How long it takes to clear an issue depends on a number of things and isn't entirely up to you, so be patient. It can take as long as a few years for some issues to clear. Meanwhile, they will become increasingly less of a problem. It's important to acknowledge your progress so that you continue with this work and don't become discouraged. There's nothing to lose and everything to gain. You'll find that this investigation is well worth it.

One thing that can undermine your determination to heal an issue is the belief that it's too difficult to heal. This belief comes from the ego, of course. The ego will try to discourage you with doubts and negative remarks: "Why bother? It won't make a difference. I just have to live with it. I just have to accept being this way. It's just the way I am." These remarks may seem harmless enough. They are the kinds of things people say to themselves all the time, but they can subtly undermine your will and determination to be free. These kinds of statements belong to the ego. It doesn't want you to be free of your conditioning because it would be out of a job.

The ego also uses fear to keep you from being free from your conditioning: "If you stop thinking you're fat, you'll probably let yourself go." "If you don't keep the house spotless, people will judge you." "If you were really happy, you probably wouldn't accomplish anything." Such beliefs are important to become aware of because the fear of those consequences can keep you from being free.

Here's a way to uncover the fears that keep your negative beliefs in place:

> *Some beliefs are held in place by fear. To release these beliefs, ask yourself, "What am I afraid will happen if I don't believe that?" Find the fears — all of them — see the falseness of those fears, and then counteract those beliefs with positive statements.*

For example, take the belief "I'll never be happy." What if you didn't believe that? One answer might be that you would try to be happy and you might fail. Having the belief that you will never be happy keeps you from having to try to be happy or having to discover what makes you happy and from the disappointment you might experience if you failed. The belief itself blocks your happiness because why would you even try to be happy if you believed you could never be happy?

Then, being an unhappy person becomes part of your identity. Who would you be if you weren't an unhappy person? Sometimes, it feels better to have any identity, even the identity of an unhappy person, than an uncertain identity. Once an idea becomes part of one's identity, people become attached to seeing themselves that way and even do things to prove it to themselves and others.

Conditioning that relates to the self-image ("I am...") keeps you tied to a certain way of thinking about yourself, which becomes comfortable because it's familiar, even if it isn't a positive way of thinking about yourself and even if it isn't very true. If you were told to think of yourself a certain way by your parents, proving them wrong might seem wrong to you. Children take on identities that others give them, even when those identities are harmful or don't fit, until they have the courage to see things differently.

Your self-image is just that, an image, an idea, nothing more. It has no power to shape you except the power you give it. If you think of yourself a certain way, your actions and words follow suit, and pretty soon others agree with your self-image.

Negative self-images, and even some positive ones, are limiting because they represent only a sliver of the truth, although when you believe them, they often become more true. To exchange a negative self-image for a truer one, you only need to see how limited and false the old image is and start believing that you are loving and good and the other qualities of your divine self.

How do you start believing something when you don't believe it? First, you simply decide to believe it. You make that intention. Then, you reinforce this intention with self-talk and self-images that represent this new sense of self. You could even create a collage of pictures that represents this new sense of self and look at it every day. Re-imaging yourself this way reprograms your subconscious. And, importantly, follow up with your actions by *acting* as your divine self would act: Be kind, attentive, patient, loving, accepting, compassionate, and courageous. Finally, you stop giving your attention to thoughts and images that undermine this new image. What you focus on, you become.

Let's take another example. The belief that you are a failure and that you'll never be successful may be the result of a self-image your parents gave you, or it may be a conclusion you came to because of some failure. Many other beliefs may be attached to it, such as: "I'm not as smart as others." "I don't have what it takes." "I don't fit in." "I don't like to work." "I need to be taken care of." "I can't handle responsibility."

There also may be fears that keep the belief that you are a failure in place: fear of failure, fear of being someone who is successful, fear of being unloved if you fail or even if you succeed, fear of responsibility, and on and on. The conclusion that you are a failure, like many other conditioned beliefs, becomes part of your self-image.

This complex of beliefs would also cause you to have any number of feelings: sadness, anger, shame, fear, or jealousy. Unfortunately, these feelings don't stay hidden very well, especially when circumstances trigger this conditioning. Such feelings can interfere with relating to others, particularly with coworkers and employers. The belief that you will never be successful also affects your body posture and actions: You act insecure, self-conscious, and unconfident, and others see this and believe what you believe about yourself. This belief, then, becomes a self-fulfilling prophecy.

What is the solution? First, you have to become aware that

you are creating the experience of being unsuccessful *in part* by your beliefs. However, it seems important to add that you aren't creating everything in your life by your beliefs, and changing your beliefs isn't going to make your life become exactly as you'd like it to be. That would be magical thinking. Changing your beliefs will only open up possibilities blocked by your negative beliefs.

By the way, is there really anything such as failure or success? Success and failure are concepts created by the ego without any intrinsic reality. These concepts are judgments on the part of the ego. From the point of view of your divine self, mistakes (what the ego calls failure) lead to learning, and learning leads to not making that mistake again. And that's progress, which can ultimately lead to what the ego experiences as success. That's the truth about life, but the ego will spin a negative tale whenever it can.

Once you are aware that you are creating the experience of feeling unsuccessful, both by how you think about your experiences and by the self-image you project, you can begin to deconstruct that self-image and replace it with a truer and more positive one. That new self-image might include "I'm someone who has grown from my mistakes" or "I'm someone who is willing to make an effort and learn" or "I have as much right to success as anyone."

Here's how to transform your negative self-images:

Take whatever negative story you've spun about yourself and spin it differently — more positively. Try to see yourself and your experience as your divine self, your soul, or a loving parent would. What would your divine self or soul say to encourage you to trust life and trust yourself and open up to new possibilities?

Examine what you've said to yourself about yourself and your life, weed out the negative statements, and find new, more positive ways of speaking about yourself and about life. Whatever leads to feeling at peace, loved, and supported is a truer statement than anything that leaves you feeling contracted, fearful, powerless, angry, or ashamed.

Next, if there are negative emotions that accompany your story about yourself, allow yourself to just be with them, one at a time, to discover the mistaken conclusions you came to that caused those feelings. Take your time doing this because it is a very important step. It's very difficult to change your conditioning when feelings keep getting triggered. You'll know you are succeeding when the negative feelings lessen and aren't triggered as often. To uncover any fears around letting go of your beliefs, ask, "What am I afraid will happen if I don't believe that?" and see what other beliefs keep that negative self-image in place.

Some of this emotional healing work can be done on your own, while very entrenched and buried beliefs and any trauma may require a therapist or other healer. One of the best methods for working with childhood issues, either on your own or with a therapist, is Inner Child work. Rather than repeating what was already explained in an earlier book by this author called *Trusting Life: Overcoming the Fear and Beliefs That Block Peace and Happiness,* I'm including an excerpt here from that book about doing this type of healing work.

Working with the Inner Child

If your trust has been damaged in childhood, it will be important to do some inquiry and other kinds of healing work around this to help restore trust. One of the most effective healing methods is Inner Child work. It's designed to heal the erroneous and usually damaging conclusions you came to as a child as a result of your upbringing and other experiences.

The child you once were lives on within you in your unconscious mind and is called the Inner Child. If your Inner Child's healthy development was impeded or arrested, you can help her (or him) grow up by meeting with her in your imagination and giving her what she needed that she didn't get. You can be the loving and wise parent she needed but may not have had and, thereby, heal any wounding that occurred.

When you do this work in your imagination, an amazing thing happens: The child who once felt unloved, unhappy, and distrustful is transformed into a child who feels loved, happy, and trusting, and then that becomes the state in which she lives on in your unconscious mind.

The effect is that a happy Inner Child won't sabotage you with negativity, fears, and doubts like an unhappy Inner Child. Many of the negative thoughts, fears, and doubts that arise in your egoic mind come from your Inner Child. When she is healed, those thoughts either disappear altogether or aren't as compelling and can be dismissed more easily.

The reason working with the Inner Child through your imagination—through images—is effective is that the memories of your childhood are stored as images, and they affect you subconsciously. When you bring these images into conscious awareness and work with them in your imagination, they are re-stored as new images, replacing the old ones, which effectively reprograms the subconscious. Since psychological complexes, like the Inner Child, are stored as images and can be accessed through the imagination, it makes sense that they can be worked with and reprogrammed through the imagination as well. Hypnotherapy works with imagery in a similar way to heal traumas and transform behaviors.

Many find they can do Inner Child work easily and safely enough on their own, although you might want to find a therapist to help you, especially if you experienced abuse as a child or if you're experiencing intense or overwhelming feelings.

To prepare to do this work, sit or lie down in a comfortable position, relax, take some time to move into a peaceful state, and affirm your willingness and readiness to receive the understanding and healing you need.

When you're ready to begin, invite your Inner Child to come forward so that you can interact with her (or him) and get to know her. Doing this work doesn't take any special skill or talent. Most people can see their Inner Child in their imagination quite easily. Can you see her in your mind's eye? What does she look like? How old is she? What is she wearing?

Your Inner Child is not an idea of yourself but a psychological complex that exists within you. When you call her forth, this complex is what you experience, not just an idea of what you were like as a child. Working with your Inner Child is not carried out on a mental level but on a psychic level.

The communication you will have with your Inner Child is a sacred one, as it is a precious opportunity to connect with an aspect of yourself that has a powerful influence on how you feel about yourself and how you operate in life. It's an opportunity to find out what conclusions she came to as a result of her experiences and how those conclusions have been influencing your feelings and behavior as an adult. It's also an opportunity to comfort and heal the Inner Child and, in so doing, heal yourself.

As part of getting to know your Inner Child, you'll have a dialogue with her. You'll ask her some questions about herself and then listen for her answers, which will come to you intuitively. When you invite material to arise from the subconscious and give it space to be received, something will show up that's pertinent to the inquiry. Dialoguing in this way requires receptivity on your part—not thinking. So, for the time being, do your best to set the thinking mind aside.

One of the most important things you want to explore with your Inner Child is what it's like to be her: How does she feel about herself? Her parents? Her friends? Life? The future?

The answers to these questions will give you a good idea of what she believes—what she has concluded about herself, other people, God, and life. For instance, if she says she feels lost and alone, what might she have concluded about herself, life, God, and others as a result of feeling that way? Any number of conclusions are possible.

These conclusions are something for you to explore at a later time through inquiry: What conclusions did your Inner Child come to as a result of feeling the way she felt or having the experiences she had? These conclusions will continue to have some influence on you as an adult, particularly if you are unaware of them. Awareness frees you from them to a great extent.

After getting to know your Inner Child some, the next step is to ask her what she needs and wants from you. Take some time to just listen and hear what she has to say. Then, tell her the things she needs to hear, the things a wise and loving parent would say to her. Be that loving, wise, and compassionate parent that she and every child deserves. Tell her things like: "I love you." "You are a beautiful child." "What happened to you wasn't fair, and it wasn't your fault; you didn't deserve it."

"You are strong and courageous to have survived." "You were just doing what children do." "You did the best you could to take care of yourself." "You are lovable and capable." "You are full of goodness." "You deserve to be happy." "You can trust life."

Tell her all the things she needs to hear so that she can relax and be happy and at peace. What will make her feel loved, happy, trusting, and at peace with herself and with life? Whatever it is that has this effect is the truth. The conclusions she came to that made her feel the opposite weren't true. They were misunderstandings on her part—the understandable but untrue conclusions that children often come to. Help her see things more clearly and truly. Help her see the truth about herself, about her parents, about life, about other people. You have the wisdom within you now to see things from another perspective, from the perspective of an adult.

Sit her on your lap, hold her, comfort her, stroke her hair in the way you would like to have been held and cared for as a child. Give her the attention, love, and affection that she needed. Be the ideal parent that she didn't have.

When this exchange feels finished, tell your Inner Child you'll be back soon to spend some time with her again. And be sure to do that, even if it's just a few minutes. Establish a relationship with your Inner Child. When you're upset about something, visit with her and see what she might have to say about it. See what you can learn from her about why you feel the way you do.

Chapter 4
Working with Ascended Masters and Guides

How to Connect with Ascended Masters and Guides

"Guide" is a term used specifically for beings who guide a soul's evolution in a reincarnational system, usually a system they graduated from and gained a great deal of knowledge and understanding of. Being a guide is an art and takes a great deal of experience beyond simply graduating from the physical plane, that is, completing the cycle of reincarnation. Those who train to be guides go through a lengthy and rigorous training under the supervision of other more advanced guides. Thus, there are both what you might call master guides, or guides that guide and train other guides, and guides who have varying levels of expertise.

Most people have three to five guides who work with them at any one time. One guide stays with you your entire lifetime and knows you completely and intimately and was probably with you in other lifetimes, while the others come and go depending on what's needed. When you undergo a big change or simply grow up or take on a new course of study or change your profession, some of your guides are likely to change.

More specialized guides that help with particular professions, talents, and life purposes will show up when needed and leave when no longer needed. Some people have pre-life agreements with certain guides or other beings to carry out specific tasks, such as writing a book, creating art, composing music, inventing something, or doing energy work or other types of healing.

The more influence a person has in the world, the more likely they are to have more than the usual number of guides. For instance, a president would have many guides, since the decisions made by him or her affect so many. However, a guide's influence is only as great as the person's receptivity. If those guides aren't listened to, it's as if that person has none. This is why electing or selecting only people of good character to be in powerful positions is especially important. People of good character obviously have some connection with their guides, while those divorced from their soul's guidance have only their ego to rely on, which is a dangerous situation.

Your guides guide you in many ways, but the primary ways are through your intuition and through inner nudges, joy, "ah-has," excitement, a sense of "yes" or "no," and other people. These ways may seem too subtle to be effective, but even souls who are less advanced find themselves responding to these cues without realizing it. Everyone follows such cues more than they realize, and becoming more aware of them will help speed up your evolution.

Through these cues, your guides are always speaking with you, suggesting things to do, directions to go in, and people and information to pay attention to. You are far from alone! You have an entire team of beings working with you whose sole task (no pun intended) is to help you learn and grow as your soul intended. They are working with you 24-7, so please know this, and that will help you become more aware of them.

Ascended Masters are beings who have gone beyond the cycle of reincarnation and advanced even further, beyond most guides, to being teachers and guides for all of humanity. Ascended Masters are not personal guides but guide the affairs on earth in a way that personal guides cannot and do not.

While personal guides help people fulfill their life purpose and learn their lessons, Ascended Masters are involved in a broader plan and design for all of humanity. Ascended Masters are orchestrating the plan for humanity, not for a single human being, although every individual's soul's plan affects this greater plan. Ascended Masters do become involved in guiding individuals at times, when their life purpose relates to humanity's evolution as a whole. For instance, I or other Ascended Masters might be involved with individuals or groups who are trying to bring about world peace or raise consciousness or teach spiritual principles or stabilize climate change.

And yet, I want to emphasize that I am available to all who call upon me, for I and other Ascended Masters are able to perform countless tasks at once and be anywhere and everywhere in the blink of an eye.

The reason for calling on Ascended Masters instead of guides might be for healing, since that is one of their roles in relation to humanity. Another might be to ask them for protection from negativity, as Ascended Masters work with angels, guides, and others to provide this for those who call upon them. They can also help bring you into alignment with your divine self when you ask for this. It is their job to help you grow and evolve, along with your guides, and they'll send energy and whatever else is needed to facilitate this growth.

You are always receiving assistance from beings in higher dimensions, but by asking, you will receive this help more fully and more often. So, that's why it's important to call upon your guides and the Ascended Masters. Your prayers and intentions signal an openness and readiness for whatever you're asking for. On the other hand, if you seem to want to go it alone, your guides and the Ascended Masters will allow you to experience whatever you're experiencing without their help, for they will not transgress your free will.

This help may come in the form of healing energy, clearing of negativity, healing of emotional wounds, insight, upliftment to a higher state of consciousness, and inspiration and ideas about how to proceed with something. Guides and Ascended Masters can also inspire others to be of help to you. Some of the most important help you receive comes from other people who are acting as instruments for guides and the Masters.

There's no special trick or formula for connecting with guides and the Ascended Masters. You simply have to sincerely ask to connect with them. This sincerity often comes out of suffering: You're struggling with something and desperately want help. However, you don't need to be struggling to ask for help. You can connect with guides and Masters throughout your day by simply making the intention to connect with them and then taking a moment to feel that connection and state whatever you'd like help with.

You can get in the habit of acknowledging the presence of guides and Masters and asking for their assistance throughout your day, and this will make a difference in how you experience life. Feeling connected in this way is the opposite of how the ego feels, which is why a practice of connecting with higher-dimensional beings regularly and frequently can be so powerful. It's a way of counteracting the ego's sense of separation and fear and distrust of life.

This is how a connection with your guides and the Ascended Masters is built—by regularly and frequently acknowledging their presence in your life and expressing your desire for them to be more present and active in your life. Although beings in higher dimensions are always available to you, the strength of that connection is determined by your intention and desire to connect with them and to have them be more actively involved in your life. The more you acknowledge them and ask for their help, the more they are available to you.

This is one of the secrets to a happy life: Invite your guides and the Ascended Masters to be more active in your life, and this will change your experience of life and change your life. To strengthen your relationship with them, you have to open the door first on your end. They're waiting for you to do this, and doing this marks another stage on the spiritual path, which will make it possible to advance more quickly and smoothly.

As I said, there is no trick to doing this, but you have to connect with guides and Masters repeatedly and regularly, because that's how those on other dimensions know of your sincerity and commitment to raising your vibration and making your spiritual growth a priority. Your sincerity is gauged by how often you consciously connect with us, and we answer that sincerity by serving you in ways you've asked for and in ways we see fit. Although there is no set formula or protocol for contacting us, I have some suggestions for how to do this. But keep in mind that your sincerity is what's most important.

First of all, you don't need to call on your guides or specific Masters by name, although you are welcome to. We know how to best serve you, and those who can best serve you will come forth and do so. You don't need to know anything about your guides or about the Ascended Masters to receive their help, although we realize that people like names and a sense of connecting with a particular being or beings, in which case ask for help from specific beings if you like and know that you'll receive it. But also know that connecting to one specific being is not important to your growth, as each of you has many beings involved with you at any one time, all serving various functions and changing roles as needed. Just know that if you seek to establish a particular relationship with one of us, that will happen, but there will also be many others involved with you who are well-equipped to serve you.

Second, you don't need to know what needs to be healed to receive healing. Just ask for healing, and it will be given as needed. Sometimes, people think they need to be specific in asking for healing: "Help me heal my relationship with my mother" for example. But it's really okay to simply ask for healing around "whatever is needed at this time." That may or may not be around your relationship with your mother or a specific issue you are aware of. These things have their own timing, although being aware of an issue and asking for help with it is certainly beneficial. My point is don't wait until you feel you need healing around a specific issue to ask for healing. On a regular basis, ask for whatever healing is most needed, and we will be able to speed up your general healing and growth.

And third, in addition to asking for general healing, ask for help in raising your consciousness, in general and in specific moments throughout your day. Throughout your day, ask for an infusion, or transmission, of higher energy to help raise your vibration. We are able to send you energy that will shift your consciousness, but you have to be open to receiving it and also make space in your life to receive it, perhaps by stopping briefly and being quiet long enough to shift your state or by taking time to meditate. Do your part by doing your best to move out of the egoic state of consciousness. Making an effort shows your sincerity. We offer what we offer, but you must be in a state of receptivity, a relaxed and open state, to receive what we have to offer.

Asking for our help is the first step in shifting your consciousness. Then, do something to back this request up, such as stating a positive affirmation or prayer that uplifts you, stopping to take a few deep breaths, noting what you're grateful for, smiling, or doing something kind for someone. Learn to raise your own vibration through positive self-talk, affirmations, being loving and sending love to others, and through reframing, or telling a more positive story about your experience than what the ego might be telling. Enlist us in your efforts to raise your vibration, and those efforts will be more effective. When we see you making efforts to heal yourself and raise your vibration, we know you are sincere and ready to move forward spiritually.

The method for connecting with us couldn't be simpler: Make an intention to connect with us, speak to us, ask for what you want in general or specifically, and then follow up by taking the steps you are able to, to heal and raise your vibration. Healing and raising your vibration are the things we can best help you with and how we can best serve you.

As far as getting you more money or more success or a partner in life, we can only do so much, since whether or not you get these and other things you want depends not only on your efforts, but on what's best for your soul's plan and its unfolding. Timing is everything, and some of what you desire might interfere with other things in your life that are meant to unfold.

Leave the unfolding of your life to your guides. They will bring you the opportunities and people you need to fulfill your lessons and life purpose. They are overseeing the unfolding of your life, and all you have to do is work with what they're bringing you or not bringing you. Sometimes, limitation, such as not having money or a relationship, is exactly the experience you need before you can have money or a particular relationship.

Trust in the unfolding of life. There is wisdom in the experiences you are having. As I have so often said, you are having the right experience, and seeing whatever you are experiencing this way is the key to not suffering. You are being watched over, guided, loved, and supported every step of the way in your life.

Please know this and feel free to connect with me and others in higher dimensions many times throughout your day. Stop and say "Hi, I know you're there and working in my highest good. Thank you for helping me today. I'm open and willing to receive whatever healing, love, insights, and guidance you might have for me."

That's all. Our instructions are very simple. Anyone who is pure of heart can and will connect with us simply by stating a desire to do so. And anyone can receive what they need from us in terms of healing, upliftment, inspiration, and insights simply by asking for these things. You may not receive everything your ego wants, unless that's good for your growth, but you will surely receive what your soul wants and needs.

The Practice of Prayer

In prayer, you hand over, or surrender, your problems, fears, and concerns to a "higher power." This is very healing. Doing this frees you from the ego's problems, fears, and concerns. They truly are just the ego's and not real in any way.

In prayer, you surrender your ego's perspective. In doing so, what remains is reality. When you drop your fears and concerns, you drop into the simple here and now. Within that are all the answers you will ever need for how to live your life. Just as a child might hand over a torn picture to her mother for mending, you hand over your broken thoughts and feelings to a higher power, and they're made right. The feeling of relaxation is how you know they've been made right.

Passing on a problem to someone else is such a relief when you know that problem is something that person can handle easily. Prayer is like that: You give your problem to a higher power to handle it for you. The truth is the problem never did exist and the higher power has been handling life perfectly all along. But to relax your ego and mind, participating in this ritual of prayer can be very helpful.

You could say that what relaxes is the animal part of you, which is fear-based. It needs to be soothed somehow so that it doesn't sabotage your life. It isn't wise, and it's churning out fearful, stress-producing, and nonproductive thoughts.

Prayer is one way to calm "the beast" within. Even if there were no spiritual forces to answer your prayers, praying would be healing for the simple reason that it calms your brain's limbic system and helps you become present, assuming you believe in prayer.

There's another reason to believe in the power of prayer: Prayer gives you the confidence that, with help, you can overcome the ego's fears and negativity. One of the ways the ego stays in control is by convincing you that it is more powerful than you are. This belief, like so many others, is a self-fulfilling prophecy. It discourages you and prevents you from accessing your innate strengths. Prayer is a way to regain access to those strengths.

A sincere prayer also summons and fortifies your will. It strengthens your resolve to be transformed, to move beyond any limiting conditioning and old habits. Prayer is a way of declaring to your unconscious mind that you intend to change. In a sense, you are giving a heads-up to your unconscious mind that, going forward, it's not business as usual.

What is the best way to pray? The sincerity of the prayer is more important than the specific words. Spiritual forces respond most strongly to fervent supplications. However, this doesn't mean you will get whatever you ask for just because you pray for it (which you've probably noticed). Life doesn't necessarily give people what they want, because it has its own plan and reasons for providing or not providing what it does.

What you can be sure of is that you'll get the help you need for dealing with whatever you're struggling with. That help may come in the form of inner strength, a book, an important idea or insight, a shift in attitude, help from a friend, or benefits in other areas of your life to ease your circumstances.

You can never pray too often. One of the mistakes people make is they think they don't need to ask a second time for something. But you do. You need to ask again and again for as long as you need to. Here's why: If you get caught in negative thoughts and feelings, spiritual forces regard that as you choosing those thoughts, since you aren't choosing to disregard them. Because spiritual forces respect your free will, they won't interfere with your choice to think those thoughts. So, if you want help with any negative thoughts and feelings, you have to ask for help whenever you need it.

When you catch yourself contracted and immersed in negative thoughts and feelings, that's the time to pray for help in shifting your consciousness. Do this diligently each time you are caught in the mind's lies, and you will see a difference. It will become increasingly easy to not get caught or not stay caught.

What follows is a general prayer for transformation that you can modify to suit your needs. Add whatever else you'd like to, to this prayer, including specifically what you want healed, what you'd like insight about, what you need acceptance for, what you want to let go of or forgive, and so on.

I am willing and ready to receive help in…

Seeing whatever needs to be seen,
Doing whatever needs to be done,
Healing whatever needs to be healed,
Understanding whatever needs to be understood,
Accepting whatever needs to be accepted,
Letting go of whatever needs letting go of,
Forgiving whatever needs to be forgiven,
Growing in whatever ways I need to grow.

When you declare such intentions, you connect with the loving forces that are guiding all of life. These forces celebrate your desire to be happier, to grow, and to be more loving and at peace. When you pray, spiritual forces come forward to do what they can to help you move in your intended direction.

One of the ways spiritual forces know you're ready for a new relationship to life is through a statement of your readiness, such as a prayer. It is a very powerful prayer, indeed, that declares your desire for freedom from ego-generated suffering. Such a prayer signals a point in your evolution when you are ready to wake up from the illusion that you are who your thoughts tell you that you are.

Prayers help you feel connected to something greater than yourself. Feeling connected in this way brings peace, and it is the truth: You are connected to and part of everything. Moreover, what you are connected to is benevolent! This understanding is so important in being able to relax and let life be as it is. You are safe. Life is good. You are love. And you are eternal. The more you know this, the easier it is to do what you need to do to be in the moment, such as to be in your body and senses, to relish the adventure of not knowing, to accept life, to be grateful, and to be loving.

The power of prayer comes, in part, from how easy it is to do. It's so easy to do that you can do it many times a day, whenever you're feeling beleaguered by the mind. People need something this easy and at their fingertips to help them overcome their relentless negative programming. A simple prayer like "Help me to accept this" or "May I be more present" might be all you need to shift out of negative thoughts.

Here are a few other suggestions for prayers that you might say in the course of your day:

> *Help me to (or May I) know what to do now.*
> *Help me to know what to say now.*
> *Help me to see the Divine in everyone.*
> *Help me to see the good in X.*
> *Help me to be more loving to X.*
> *Help me to quiet my mind.*
> *Help me to be happy.*
> *Help me to let go.*
> *Help me to be patient.*

Making a prayerful statement stops the egoic mind in its tracks and replaces its words with words that help you step outside the mind. Prayer is a way of snatching the reins from the ego. Prayer can help you become more established in the moment and less at the mercy of your negative programming.

Why Prayer Is Healing

Prayer is healing in many ways. For one thing, it identifies the issue, the problem, or the need—the thing you feel is missing that makes you unhappy. To pray for help, you need to be aware of something you want changed. This awareness is the first step in changing something. Awareness empowers you to change whatever you would like to change. It also enables you to get assistance from your guides and the Ascended Masters to do that.

So, when you pray, two things are happening: You are asking for assistance from other realms and calling it forth. But importantly, you are also defining for yourself what you want on a deeper level. What is it you think you need or want to be happy?

When you speak your needs, you may discover they aren't true needs and that there is something deeper that is more important to pray for. When you open yourself up to speaking to your guides and the Ascended Masters, an evolution can happen. You discover things about yourself. This is the basis for psychotherapy as well, or the value of friendship and relationship. When you speak things out loud, you learn about yourself. So, it is with prayer: You learn about yourself. Things that are unconscious become conscious. Your awareness grows.

Prayer is also a way of reprogramming the subconscious and helping you move forward. You form an intention, state that intention, and that creates a new possibility. Perhaps you've been following some habit that hasn't been helpful. When you speak an intention to change that habit, your subconscious mind aligns with that and says: "Okay, now that I know what you want, let's do that. I thought you wanted the other thing."

The same is true of the forces assisting you in other dimensions. When they hear of your intention, they come forward and say: "Okay, she's ready to have something new in her life. She's ready for help. She's finally aware of this and ready for us to help her with it." That's what goes on when you pray.

When you pray, it's good to say whatever you are moved to say, to get it out in the open, where you can see it. Then, you can see if it is true or not. Sometimes, you hold back your thoughts instead of examining them, and in holding them back, they persist. If you have a negative belief, it won't stop coming up until it is acknowledged and examined. It won't be healed unless you see it and examine it, and in that examination, see that it isn't true.

It isn't enough to be aware of a negative thought if you still believe it. You have to be aware of it and also see that it isn't true. Only then, can you be free of it. Just being aware of a negative thought—just witnessing it—is not enough to heal it. If a thought is still believed, it will come up again, although witnessing does diminish its strength, and witnessing is better than identifying with it. Identifying with a negative thought would be believing it and reinforcing it by speaking it.

If you want to be free of a thought, you have to question its validity. If you do, you will always discover that a negative thought is not true, that it isn't valid. A true thought would be true under all circumstances and true always, because that is what truth is. Truth is true. Given this, very few thoughts would pass this test.

If a thought that makes you feel bad doesn't pass this test, isn't true always and throughout time, then what good is it? It has no useful purpose. It only makes you feel bad. So, you can discard it. To move beyond negative beliefs and misunderstandings, you have to really, truly see that they are useless and untrue. When you stop believing them, they will diminish in their power and arise much less frequently.

In speaking out loud to your guides and the Ascended Masters, you are speaking these thoughts. Doing this, is like writing in a journal. You can see what's in your mind, what falseness is there. Speak your thoughts, listen to yourself, see the falseness, and see what is true. You will know when you are speaking truth in a prayer because of how it feels.

Talking to your guides and the Ascended Masters is a little bit like therapy. You're talking to wise, accepting, compassionate beings, who are truly loving you unconditionally. This is a powerful experience, as is therapy for many people when it's done properly. Having a compassionate, accepting being witnessing your life, witnessing your thoughts and your expression, is very powerful, very healing. Then, you can begin to sort out what's true and isn't true, what's real and isn't real, what you want and what you don't really want, what you need and what you don't really need.

Prayer is an exercise in emotional health and well-being. Do this for yourself. Prayer can be part of a natural clearing process you can engage in every day. Talk to your guides and the Ascended Masters, and you will never feel alone, for they are always there listening. More and more, you will begin to experience that they are always there and always loving you, always caring. For those of you who didn't have proper parenting, this type of relationship is like being reparented.

When you express your needs to your guides and the Ascended Masters and those needs are fulfilled on the deepest levels, sometimes apparently and sometimes less apparently, there is much less need for others to fulfill your needs. Because you receive what you need within yourself from this relationship, there is less need to speak to others about your needs, who sometimes are not that helpful. Human beings can often reinforce negative thoughts and egoic ways of thinking. You won't find that when talking to higher forces.

Like any relationship, a relationship with your guides and the Ascended Masters is something that must be nurtured over time. But time spent in prayer is time well spent, as this relationship will support you and give you a sense of stability and wholeness, completeness.

What You Receive When You Pray

Just as important as speaking to God is listening to God. When you listen to God, you listen with your whole self. You aren't listening with your ears, because you aren't likely to receive words in answer to your questions. But your Heart will receive answers. Your body will receive answers. You will receive knowings, a sense of rightness, courage, strength, inspiration, and ideas.

When you open up this line of communication with God, you open yourself up to more of what has already been given to you to help you along your way. The beings that are guiding your life can activate your strength and courage. They can drop an inspiration or idea into your body or mind. They can steer you here or there with feelings of excitement and joy. These are the answers you receive when you develop a relationship to God in prayer.

You may not receive these "answers" as soon as you ask for them, though. They are scattered throughout your day. You never know when you might receive an answer. All of a sudden you have an answer or an inspiration. All of a sudden you have an idea, you feel strength, you feel excitement, you feel joy, or you feel connected. These are the answers to your prayers. Life brings you the people you need, the opportunities you need, and the ideas and inspiration you need.

Life brings you everything you need—and nothing more. You aren't brought things you don't need. That could be confusing and throw you off-track. Other people might bring you opportunities, but if they aren't aligned with your greatest good, they probably won't work out or you won't feel like pursuing them. So, if life brings you an opportunity and you are joyful and excited about it, then by all means, say yes to it, because it must be right. Opportunities are answers to your prayers, whether or not you recognize them as that.

When you pray, you always receive something, but if you don't notice what you are receiving, it is as if you haven't received it. For instance, if you receive strength, and you don't recognize the strength inside yourself, it is as if you don't have it. Or if you recognize the strength but talk yourself out of it, it is as if it hasn't been given to you.

It is important to recognize these gifts, or you won't use them. You won't feel that you have them. You will close down and think you don't have the support you need, and the egoic fears will take over. You have to work at noticing and acknowledging the subtle gifts that are available to you and also the opportunities that are not so subtle.

Acknowledging these things doesn't come naturally, because the mind doesn't acknowledge subtle realities, such as courage, faith, love, strength, and patience. The egoic mind doesn't view these as significant. It sees the world from a place of lack. Even when you have been given gifts, the egoic mind often doesn't see them, accept them, or utilize them. It sees right past them and goes on thinking that there isn't enough, that this is a limited universe, that "I never get what I want. I can't seem to get what I need. The world is against me." This is the egoic perception. You are programmed to feel lacking inside and to feel the world is lacking, unkind, threatening, and that you have to fight to survive.

These beliefs, themselves, create this reality. Believing that the world is a fearful place and that goodness is not behind life, but difficulty and perhaps even evil, will create that very experience. These beliefs become a self-fulfilling prophecy. The mind creates its own reality by believing certain things. You become your own worst enemy when you believe your thoughts.

The thoughts in your thought-stream are not your friend. They don't have your best interest at heart. They don't give you courage or strength or patience—they do the opposite, don't they? The thoughts in your head take away your courage, your strength, and your patience. They make you irritable, impatient, unhappy, and feeling like a victim. How are these thoughts your friend? How are they helpful? Why do you listen to them?

And so, you have to learn to listen on a more subtle level to the gifts that appear there. You have to learn to notice the courage, the strength, the patience, the perseverance, and all the other qualities you innately have by virtue of being a divine being: "As above, so below."

The Divine is goodness, and this goodness is within you. This goodness is not so accessible at times because your egoic mind is your default. The egoic mind nullifies these gifts. It neutralizes them. It disempowers you. So, you have to learn to move beyond the mind to regain your power as a divine son or daughter. You have all the goodness, all the strength, and everything you need to live this life beautifully, happily, joyfully, and to be of service to all of creation in the way you are meant to be. You have everything you need to be this in the world. You have to overcome the egoic mind, though, which interferes with knowing this and tapping into these gifts from God, which are qualities of your divine nature.

So, the key is to notice the gifts: Notice the courage, notice the love, notice the patience, notice the strength and the abilities to persevere, to care, and to connect with others. Everything that is good about human beings is your divine nature. So, dear ones, notice how wonderful you are. Notice your goodness, notice your strength, and know that they are gifts given to you to help you on your way and help you live the life you are meant to live. These are your resources.

You have not been left alone and you are not lacking in any way. You always have whatever you need. So, know this and know that praying will help you receive what you need and help you notice that you have received it, because once you have asked for something, you will be looking to receive it. Prayer helps you notice what you are receiving and *that* you are receiving on a continual basis.

Much more about prayer is available on a playlist on this author's YouTube channel, which is called "Gina Lake Channeling Jesus": https://bit.ly/prayerpl

How Guides Use Signs and Symbols to Guide You

Many of you are already aware that your guides on other dimensions guide you at times through signs and symbols. This is one way they might communicate with you, besides your general intuition. I'd like to explore this a little with you and help you understand how this works in your life.

Some people receive guidance through signs and symbols a lot, while others rarely do. Whether you receive guidance this way depends not only on your receptivity to receiving guidance in this form, but also on your "style," if you will, of receiving intuitive information.

Some people receive intuitive information most easily through their subtle energy body. Their subtle energy body receives or records energetic information from their environment and those around them, and that energy is translated into an intuition or insight. These are empaths: They feel what others are feeling emotionally and even physically. Other people's emotions and sensory data register in their own body. If this mode of intuiting is not fully developed, however, they may sense energy but not be able to intuit the meaning of what they're sensing.

Others receive intuitive information most easily auditorily, as in clairaudience, or channeling. They receive information directly as words in their minds. If this mode of intuiting is not fully developed, they may hear only a word or phrase here and there rather than full sentences and paragraphs, and they may have difficulty distinguishing between the voice in their head and these occasional clairaudient messages.

Those who receive intuitive information most easily visually are the ones most likely to respond to signs and symbols, since these rely on the sense of sight: You *see* something, and it triggers an intuition or insight, either immediately or later. Those who easily receive information visually also may receive information through mental pictures or symbols in their mind's eye and possibly in dreams. When this ability is full developed, it's called clairvoyance. These individuals naturally take to symbols systems such as Tarot cards and astrology, whose symbols trigger intuitive insights.

Your guides will communicate with you in whatever way or ways work best for you and whatever way is likely to work at the particular time they want to communicate something. They might use signs, symbols, or synchronicities if you're someone who pays attention to these things and when that fits. Alternately, guides might use another person as a mouthpiece if that's possible, or they might use dreams if you're someone who pays attention to dreams. But the most common way your guides communicate with you is through your intuition—you just suddenly know something, without the need for a sign or symbol. Signs and symbols simply make it easier for some people to receive an intuitive message. Everyone has some capacity for receiving information intuitively.

When guides use symbols, those symbols will be ones that are personally meaningful to you. For example, if you sailed when you were young and have associations with sailing, then a toy sailboat, an actual sailboat, a picture of a sailboat, a book or even a song about sailing might be used to trigger a memory, a feeling, an insight, something you learned, or an association you formed around sailboats that's useful to you in the present moment. For instance, if sailing was a particularly happy memory, then your guides directing your attention to a sailboat might be their way of bringing up those happy feelings. Sometimes, guides simply remind you of what makes you happy or what you might need to be happy. Maybe it's time to go sailing!

Or if you've heard that 11:11 or some other number is a way that your guides communicate with you, then your guides might try to get your attention by making you aware of this number in your environment. Your guides are able to steer your attention to some extent. They can often get you to notice a number or whatever they'd like you to notice. In this case, the message isn't in the number but just a way that your guides communicate, "I'm here. Pay attention." Or, for instance, if someone told you "33 means x," then your guides might use that number to communicate whatever you believe that means.

Your guides can also get you to turn on the radio or notice the words of a song being played in a store, for instance, if they want to communicate something to you through a song. Guides use songs quite often to convey an insight, remind you of something, or simply uplift your vibration. Just as easily, your guides can get you to notice a bird's song or the fragrance of a flower or something else going on in the here and now. In this way, your guides often try to point you back into your body and senses when you're lost in thought.

Symbols are very individualized communications, just as they are in dreams. When guides use symbols to communicate with you, they choose ones that are likely to be meaningful to you and ones you're likely to understand. For example, a snake in one person's dream might symbolize something quite different than a snake in another person's dream, although many common symbols, such as a snake, also have a generally understood meaning. Still, it's important to view symbols from a personal lens, not just their usual interpretation.

One of the problems with guides communicating through symbols and through signs is that someone who's learning that guides do this might assume that something they see or something that happens is a communication from guides and either not know what it means or misinterpret it. Just because guides communicate this way at times doesn't mean that everything you see is some kind of communication or that everything that happens is a sign.

Symbols and signs are meant to trigger an intuition about something, either immediately or later, not get you spinning around in your head trying to figure out what something means. That would be counterproductive. If a sign is to be useful to you, it has to trigger an intuitive understanding of what's being communicated. If not, then it's failed as a means of communication.

While symbols often communicate something specific, like an insight, a sign is often a warning. Little things going wrong might be a sign to be more careful when the potential is there for something bigger to go wrong. For instance, a small animal running across the road might alert you to the potential for a larger animal, such as a deer, crossing the road. The small animal reminds you of a bigger danger, so you proceed more cautiously.

Your guides are able to keep you out of harm's way by manipulating your attention and by slowing you down or speeding you up or getting you to change your direction. Guides are working with everyone all the time, orchestrating the dance of life, although they aren't always able to prevent accidents from happening. Nevertheless, they're usually able to minimize the impact of an accident, if not prevent one that isn't to your benefit in terms of your growth, lessons, and life purpose.

Guides provide protection at every point during your day unless you need to have a particular experience for your growth. This is why we often say, "You are having the right experience, and it's best to see things this way." Even when an accident or unintended event happens, your soul can nearly always use that experience for your growth, and your soul, through your guides, will bring you what you need to help you grow from it.

Unfortunately, when some hear that guides use signs to communicate, they sometimes take this teaching too far and assume that anything unusual, unexpected, or unwanted is a sign. If a bird grazes your windshield, what does that mean? Or if a tree is blown over in your yard during a storm, what does that mean? Events such as these may be signs, but they are more often just life happening as it does.

Being in the flow doesn't mean you won't sometimes have experiences you'd rather not have, such as root canals, broken dishes, flat tires, and all the other little troublesome things in life that happen unexpectedly. Such things usually are *not* a sign that you're out of the flow or that you somehow deserve this experience or that you brought this on yourself by something you did or something you thought.

While karma does delivers needed lessons, many of the smaller challenges in life are just the way it is on this physical plane. Things break and get old, and then you have to deal with that. When you're in the flow, dealing with such things is no big deal, as there is no resistance to taking care of such things and you don't take such things personally, meaning you don't tell a story about these things happening that makes you feel bad.

Unpleasant and even scary things happen to everyone, not necessarily because they have imperfect thoughts or bad karma but because life on earth can't be any other way. Life is challenging for everyone. The ego fantasizes that it could have perfect control over life by perfecting oneself. It fantasizes that if you were more perfect and had all positive thoughts, nothing challenging or scary would ever happen to you, but that's just not true. No matter how "spiritual" you are, you'll still have to live with a certain amount of unpleasant events. These, too, are part of the flow.

Some of life's little challenges—most likely only a few—may be signs or warnings, but unless these little challenges are accompanied by a clear intuition of what they mean, it won't be useful to see them as signs. Furthermore, it isn't useful to get overly involved in trying to figure out what something might mean with your mind. The mind doesn't have the answers to such things, and the mind is more likely than not to come to the wrong conclusion or one that makes you feel wrong or bad.

Guides are very gentle in their messages. They send signs that trigger a reminder or cause you to think of something you need to consider. Your guides may warn you through a sign, but they won't do this in a way that would scare you. You are always loved and watched over lovingly. Guides ease the way with their signs, symbols, and intuitions and help your life go more smoothly as best they can.

A Guided Meditation for Meeting Your Guide and Receiving Guidance

I want to take you on a journey inward, where you will meet one of your spirit guides who has a message for you. It will be what you most need to hear right now. We'll travel a little ways in your imagination, but know that not everything you see or experience on this journey is your imagination but, rather, an experience on another dimension, one that is far more fluid than this earthly dimension but no less real.

Where your guides reside is more beautiful than you can imagine and also more accessible than you may imagine. The journey we are taking isn't actually a long journey at all. Your guides are right here, by your side, but in another dimension that you aren't capable of seeing with your ordinary eyes. So, I will have you close your eyes and use another sense—your sixth sense—to experience one of your guides as he or she exists in a higher dimension.

So, get very comfortable, close your eyes, relax, and allow me to guide you to this meeting with your guide. You will have to do a little climbing up hill, as your guide is off the beaten path and in a remote and pristine area high on a mountain top that is strewn with flowers, an alpine meadow of enormous beauty. So, let's begin our journey.

You embark on this journey with a sense of sacredness because you know that you are about to meet a being who has been a precious resource to you in this lifetime: your lifetime guide. This guide has been with you since your first breath and knows you more intimately than any other being. This guide knows your every thought and feeling and everything you have ever experienced in this lifetime and in others.

This guide is looking forward to having you experience him or her more personally and has taken on a particular guise in which to appear to you. But know that this guide is not as he or she may appear to be but more of an embodiment of love, which is true of all who guide humanity. We are not so unique on this level, although we can appear so. Rather, we are energy beings with a unique signature but no particular identity or individuality. We are identified by our service to you, by our role in relation to you, but at our core, those who guide humanity are essentially the same.

Today, you will meet your lifetime guide in a particular appearance, and you may receive a name and a message or answer to a question. Both the appearance and the name are to help you identify your guide and helpful in relating to him or her in the future. So, let us begin.

The trek up the mountain is fairly long but not one that is overly difficult for you. As you slowly ascend this mountain, you notice that the path you are on is narrow but well-trodden, safe, and infused with light, as if your way is being lit by some mysterious energy source. You know that if you simply stay on this lighted path, you will safely and comfortably reach your destination. This path, although it is upward and takes some effort to climb, also feels effortless because you are carried along by a joy in your Heart, a sense of wonder, and a sense of excited anticipation of this fortuitous meeting.

As you continue your climb, you notice the beauty around you. The light is not only coming from the path you're walking on, but the scenery is also infused with a kind of unearthly light, the likes of which you've never before seen. And the colors are different somehow: The green is fresher, the blue is crisper, and the flowers are more alive than any flowers you've ever seen before. It is the most perfect day to meet your guide, and you feel a joyfulness and fullness inside in anticipation of this meeting.

As you continue slowly climbing up this mountain, you sense a heightened state of consciousness. You feel freer and more at peace than ever before. You have left behind any concerns related to your life and are fully in your body and senses, as is natural when you're happy and glad to be doing what you're doing.

In a little while, you'll be reaching the summit. You can almost see it now, and as you approach, you feel some excitement in your chest, like when you're about to meet someone you love and haven't seen for a very long time. That is what this is like, for you have known this guide in so many other lifetimes, and there's nothing but love and respect between you.

There are now only a hundred or so steps left in this journey before you arrive at your destination. What will you see when you reach the top? You have no idea, and not knowing this is deliciously exciting. A few more steps, and you'll be there.

Take those last steps now. You are almost at the top... And then you are there! At the top! You look around and see that you're on a rather large plateau, one that reaches infinitely, it seems, in all directions. This plateau is also strewn with flowers of every color. The light at this elevation is golden and luminescent.

The air is different here too and the colors are different here, as they were on the path. You are definitely not in Kansas anymore! This place feels very safe, very sacred, still, peaceful, like a heaven on earth—or is this even earth? It feels like no place you've ever been or seen. Take a moment to look around, orient yourself, and take in the beauty. Very soon, your guide will appear, but for now just let yourself experience this place of supreme beauty and peace...

As you await your guide, you find a comfortable place to sit and rest. You feel completely relaxed and at peace within yourself. You're happy for this time to gather and prepare yourself for this meeting. There's one particular question you've been wanting to ask your guide, so take a moment to formulate this question in your mind...

Then, you notice a figure moving toward you. It's your guide! As your guide glides toward you, you can't take your

Working with Ascended Masters and Guides

eyes off this figure. The beauty, the grace, the compassion, and the love are expressed with every movement and every look.

As your guide approaches, you stand up in greeting and look into your guide's eyes for the answer to your question. Take a moment now to telepathically receive that answer and also to take in your guide's love and blessing…

When you feel finished communing with your guide, you say thank you. Your guide reminds you that you are welcome to call upon him or her any time for help, consolation, upliftment, information, guidance, or whatever else you might need. Know that this is a true experience and one you can have again any time you feel you need something from your guide, whether that is an answer to a question or comfort or support.

Your guide gives you a solid hug, and you are filled with love and light. As your guide retreats, you wave and turn back toward the path and begin your descent down the mountain. The descent is just as beautiful as the climb, only much easier, as you feel lighter, freer, and loved to the depths of your being. You will remember this feeling always, and when you need to feel this way again, you'll be able to recall it, and this remembrance will fill you with whatever you need. Know that you can go back to this sacred place any time and ask any other questions you might have or just commune silently with your guide. Just rest in this feeling of completeness for a while…

To listen to this guided meditation, go to Gina's YouTube channel:
https://youtu.be/WYHps2mG298

If you'd like to develop your intuition and ability to connect with help and helpers in other dimensions, see Gina Lake's and Jenai Lane's 8-week, self-directed online course "Living

Intuitively: Develop Your Connection to Your Soul's Wisdom and to Angels, Masters, and Guides":

https://radicalhappiness.com/online-courses/living-intuitively

Chapter 5
What Physical Healing Is All About

How Physical Issues Serve the Soul

The need for physical healing is a call to grow emotionally or spiritually. It is rare for emotional or spiritual issues to *not* be at the root of physical illnesses or disabilities, so it's best to assume that if you are experiencing a need for physical healing, then emotional or spiritual growth is being called for and will be integral to becoming well. Either the soul is using physical issues to grow spiritually in some way, or emotional wounds (from this lifetime or a previous one) are creating a persistent negative state that results in physical issues. The negative state may be caused by repressed anger or an ongoing state of anger, fear, grief, guilt, hatred, or remorse over an extended period of time. Negative emotions, particularly fear, anger, and grief, are literally toxic to the body and are a factor in most diseases and imbalances in the body.

First, I'd like to address physical issues that are serving a spiritual purpose. What I mean by this is that a physical challenge may be chosen by the soul prior to life as a catalyst for growth in that lifetime. There are certain qualities, divine qualities, that every soul is required to develop, such as love, patience, responsibility, compassion, courage, fortitude, perseverance, humility, and sensitivity to others; and physical challenges are often the means for developing these qualities.

And then, there is the biggest spiritual lesson of all: overcoming egoic tendencies, such as the tendency to grasp toward the future, to be greedy and never satisfied, to feel lacking and fearful, to want to be special and feel superior, to want control, and to lust for power or money or fame, to name a few.

Being ill or disabled is your ego's worst nightmare because it is very difficult for the ego to get the things it wants under these circumstances. Being ill or disabled puts people in a position of less power, not more; less control, not more; and makes it difficult to engage in worldly activities. Being ill or disabled takes you out of your normal life, roles, and identities and forces you to be less active, to stop pursuing the ego's goals, to surrender to what *is*, and to be in a position of not knowing what comes next.

This is exactly what the ego does *not* want. However, it's precisely because the ego doesn't get what it wants that illness and disability have the potential to be so spiritually transformative. These experiences can transform you from an ego-dominated human being to one who is surrendered and living moment to moment. And what you discover in this surrender is who you really are.

As you've probably noticed, it's difficult to discover your true nature, your divine nature, and live as that when you are participating fully in the world and all of its activities, especially when most people in the world are ego-identified and spending most of their time striving for what the ego wants and jockeying for positions in society.

There is nothing wrong with living this way; it's perfectly appropriate for most souls on Earth to be ego-identified and going after what the ego wants. However, there comes a time in everyone's spiritual growth for waking up from the ego. One of the most efficient ways for the soul to shift from ego-identification to living in the present moment is illness or disability.

I know this sounds strange, as going from ego-identification to waking up to your true self seems like a very big leap, but many people have experienced just that as a result of the limitations brought on by illness or disability. The circumstances are in some ways similar to being on an extended spiritual retreat, where you aren't allowed to participate in the world or in your thoughts in the usual way.

There are so many things you learn from illness and disability that you would never be able to learn any other way, not even on a spiritual retreat. To the soul, illness and disability are wonderful opportunities to grow quickly and efficiently in certain ways, primarily in compassion, but in other ways as well: patience, inner strength, courage, perseverance, and humility, to name a few. That is what I mean by spiritual growth.

Every soul must develop these qualities before graduating from the third dimension, which is why every soul chooses circumstances of illness and disability again and again in many different lifetimes to grow in these ways. A person doesn't learn these things in just one lifetime, so every soul experiences many instances of illness and disability, sometimes even in just one lifetime.

If you are experiencing an illness, a disease, or a physical limitation, then it's best to assume that that is the right experience, meaning that your soul chose this experience to grow in ways that it couldn't have without that experience. It's also possible that some emotional wounding might be behind that experience as well. Spiritual growth and emotional growth are often intertwined.

Emotional wounding that results in illness or disease is also often a choice on the part of the soul. The soul may choose to come into a family that is likely to be neglectful or abusive because it wants to grow spiritually or because this serves the soul's life purpose or both, as in the case of someone who's life purpose is to be a healer or to serve in some other compassionate way.

A life purpose related to healing or service nearly always involves an early wounding and the need to heal oneself first. For example, if your life purpose relates to healing eating issues, then your soul may choose an early environment that wounds you and results in eating issues. This wounding provides the impetus for your life purpose. So, even emotional wounding, which may or may not lead to physical issues, is usually a choice on the part of the soul because it serves a person's spiritual growth or life purpose.

Your wounds are not your fault! And your physical illnesses and disabilities are not your fault! They were chosen or designed by your soul so that you could have exactly the experience you are having, which is purposeful for your soul. Even if your physical issues are caused by overeating, for example, it's not your fault you struggle with this tendency. There is a reason you overeat, an emotional reason, either from this lifetime or another. You are here, then, to discover and uncover that wound and heal it and perhaps help others heal from a similar wound, if not in this lifetime, then in a subsequent one.

Years or lifetimes spent dealing with illnesses or disabilities are not a waste, which is what the ego feels, but valuable experiences that can catapult the soul forward significantly in its evolution. Those who choose such experiences are often on an evolutionary fast-track. And, in most cases, evolving quickly in this way is a choice, not a requirement.

Extremely challenging physical illnesses and disabilities are nearly always a choice on the part of a strong, older soul to grow exponentially. The individual, once in the body, might feel inferior or victimized as a result of such an experience, but it was a bold and heroic choice on the part of that soul, usually made to evolve quickly and to acquire empathy and other skills necessary to serve others in later lifetimes.

To blame or look down on yourself or feel bad about a physical challenge if you find yourself in this situation would only be to delay your spiritual progress. Self-pity or low self-esteem or any number of other negative feelings that the ego might produce under these circumstances are the challenges that must be overcome to reap the spiritual rewards of this choice.

A younger soul, one who is less capable of getting beyond the ego's perspective and making lemonade out of lemons, would be cautioned not to choose such a challenge. There are many other less challenging ways that a younger soul can begin to develop the inner strength and compassion needed to take on a larger challenge. Souls choose challenges that stretch them but don't break them. Granted, sometimes a soul does "bite off more than it can chew," but that is the exception, not the rule, and usually the result of not heeding the advice of one's guides.

There are many examples of disabled people becoming advocates or heroes for other disabled people because of their inner strength and ability to mentally and emotionally overcome their disability, if not their actual disability. And sometimes, incredible perseverance and belief in oneself can actually overcome a disability, for example, when someone is not expected to be able to walk again but through many hours of arduous physical therapy does.

Such individuals become an inspiration to others in their same situation. They model the personal growth and victories possible even under these circumstances. To achieve such feats takes great inner strength, patience, courage, confidence, and a positive outlook, all of which are developed further by the soul through such an experience. A soul that is already strong in these ways may take on a physical challenge in order to become even stronger and to be this kind of a model for others.

A physical challenge also may be chosen by a soul after spending many lifetimes developing physical strength and prowess as an athlete. Souls develop specific talents by repeatedly exercising certain skills lifetime after lifetime, which can result in exceptional gifts. However, this one-pointed pursuit can also result in underdevelopment in other areas, such as compassion, sensitivity to others, or empathy. When something comes easily to you because you've practiced it for lifetimes, there can be a tendency to think less of others who aren't as talented. In other words, one's ego can get carried away and a person may feel special or above others.

When this happens to a soul, especially if those talents have been physical ones, the soul might choose a lifetime with some physical challenges to develop greater empathy and humility. A lifetime of physical dependency on others, for instance, would be a very dramatic way of balancing this, but there are many other ways.

The point is that the soul makes choices that are not only for the good of the soul, but for the good of the Whole. The soul is interested in you becoming the best human being you can be—in having the best character, not necessarily the best talents. That's what life is about—becoming a good person, and you all know what I mean by this. Physical challenges have the potential for developing the qualities of your divine self.

What happens when you become ill or suddenly disabled? I've said that this is a tragedy for the ego, but it is a beautiful opportunity for the soul, because what happens when you become ill or disabled is that you no longer can go after what the ego wants and you often don't have what the ego wants either. This is a blessing in disguise.

The blessing is that illnesses or disabilities often do away with the future your ego imagined for itself. It was always only an imagined future, nothing real, but still, this is painful—to the ego. You thought you were in control of where your life was going, and now you see that you aren't.

This is a blessing because it sets you on a search to answer all sorts of questions: "What does it mean if I'm not in control of my life? Is this God's doing? Is there a God? Why is this happening to me? And how will I deal with this pain?" When the ego fails in its guidance and is proven to be not so wise or to not have answers to your questions, you begin to look elsewhere. When physical issues arise, so do the big questions in life: "Why me? Why this?" And the person either wallows in the ego's self-pity and victimhood or becomes a seeker of the Truth.

This kind of pain and uncertainty brought on by illness, disease, or disability is one of the main reasons people step onto the spiritual path or return to being a seeker after falling away for a while. Prolonged illness and disability are powerful catalysts for spiritual growth. The suffering caused by the ego under these circumstances causes people to search for the truth about how to be happy, how to be at peace, how to accept their circumstances and, importantly, how to get healed.

The healing journey is a complex one, in part because people in today's world don't know that much about healing. They tend to approach healing from a medical or scientific standpoint, which results more in treating symptoms than the whole person or getting at the cause of the difficulty, which is usually emotional or spiritual. For some, the cause is diet, but even that isn't always adequately addressed, and in any event, why the person uses food as he or she does is not usually addressed adequately.

Changing your diet is difficult without also addressing the issue of emotional eating. People overeat and eat the wrong foods for a number of reasons. Sometimes, overeating is a reaction to a lifetime or lifetimes of starvation or food scarcity. This is more common than you may realize. Other times, overeating is simply a bad habit established in childhood or a habit of eating foods, such as sugar, that are literally addictive.

But even in these cases, there is usually an emotional component: People eat to reward themselves, to try to become happy when they aren't, to relieve stress rather than address that stress or change what they're doing, to try to get energy when they're tired or over-working, and to avoid feeling certain feelings, such as anger or sadness. When overeating or eating unhealthy foods becomes daily and habitual, the body can become imbalanced and start to break down.

The ego, through the voice in your head, is what causes people to push themselves when they need rest, to eat purely for pleasure, to look to food for happiness, to soothe themselves or indulge themselves as a reward, and to stuff their anger or grief rather than process it appropriately, not to mention that people don't even know how to process their feelings.

The voice in the head runs most people's lives. It tells you what to do, how and when to do it, how fast to do it, and evaluates your every move. People don't think to question this voice because everyone around them is marching to this same drummer without questioning it. You aren't trained to do anything other than this, so it seems there is no other way to live. But the ego is a cruel and an unwise taskmaster, and while it may get things done and accomplish great feats, this is often at a great physical, emotional, and spiritual cost, and who's to say that just as much can't be done without following this voice?

What you discover when you stop listening to the voice in your head is that you get done what needs getting done and you also live a balanced life, one that includes sufficient rest and exercise, healthy food choices, and room for loved ones, creativity, fun, and other meaningful activities. When you stop listening to the voice in your head, you relax and naturally flow from one activity to the next in a way that is both efficient and enjoyable.

Your divine self knows how to live this life, and it will move you in ways you need to be moved and also include enough rest and rejuvenating activities, such as walking in nature, to keep you in tune with it. There's a different way to live than the life most people live. I will refer you to another book by this author called *From Stress to Stillness: Tools for Inner Peace* for more about how to live this way.

Physical illnesses and disabilities serve the soul's evolution in another way by providing growth through dependency on others. There are many reasons why a soul might choose the experience of dependency. Many basic spiritual qualities are developed by this experience once dependency is accepted and any sense of victimhood is overcome.

Acceptance is the first and most important quality to be developed, as developing the other qualities of your true nature depend on accepting your situation. Compassion and empathy are the most obvious other qualities developed by dependency, but not nearly the only ones. For example, those who depend on the help of others because of an illness or disability need to learn to ask for help and receive it, which isn't easy for those who've had many lifetimes of being very independent and self-sufficient.

Learning to receive is part of learning to love. Your very first relationship, the most primal one, to your mother was one of receiving. If this relationship was damaged, then receiving love and support from others will be difficult, and that inability to be open to receiving from others will be an impediment to your relationships and to feeling connected to God, if you will, and receiving love and help from beings in higher dimensions.

To receive love or help from others requires trusting someone enough to allow that person into your life. When you accept help from another, you are in relationship to that person, and that becomes an opportunity to learn to love, perhaps to love someone you wouldn't ordinarily choose to love.

Being dependent on someone physically, as is often the case when you are ill or disabled, creates a bond, and whether that bond is one of love and gratitude or shame and resentment is up to you. Are you grateful for their assistance, or do you resent their freedom and power over you or feel ashamed? How you relate to those who care for you is a choice. Do you choose love or the resentment or shame of the ego? Are you grateful, or do you take your pain out on others?

Relationships with one's caretakers are complicated ones, but they're often some of the most important bonds a soul will form. It's not uncommon for two souls in this situation to choose to continue building that bond of love between them by becoming family members in future lifetimes.

Once compassion and empathy are gained by the soul, a drive to serve others often follows. Many souls choose numerous lifetimes of dependency and then go on to choose lifetimes of serving those who are dependent, such as invalids, the mentally ill, or children, or serving in other ways. Many people's later life purposes relate to service of some sort, although some souls also choose to serve in their earlier lifetimes because they find service rewarding.

There are many lessons as well that come with serving others, such as learning to serve others appropriately — without giving so much of yourself that you are drained, demoralized, and unhappy, and without making others dependent on you. When do you help, and when do you encourage someone to help themselves?

Another extremely important quality developed through dependent lifetimes and also lifetimes of poverty, subservience, or oppression is humility. What is humbled is, of course, the ego. When you can't get what your ego wants, whether that's attention, power, money, or fame, that's humbling. You see that something more powerful than your ego is at play in life, and that's the truth. In some lifetimes, the ego is allowed to obtain the things it wants, and those lifetimes might result in hubris, narcissism, insensitivity, and a sense of specialness that needs to be balanced by experiencing the opposite of getting what your ego wants.

Lifetimes of dependency may be chosen by the soul to gain the humility needed to accomplish great things without great pride and selfishness. At the end of your lifetimes, it's possible to know yourself as the instrument of Grace through which great things are accomplished, while credit is given where credit is due. You see correctly that anything you accomplish is not really *your* accomplishment at all but God's will in action, and without the hand of Grace, you couldn't have accomplished anything. You accomplish nothing without the entire web of life being involved.

I hope you understand that no experience you have ever had in any of your lifetimes has been punishment. If you are prideful in one lifetime and choose humbling circumstances in another, that isn't punishment for your pride but a necessary balancing, one that every soul experiences at some point.

Your soul is as glad to take on a humbling experience as an exalted one. Your soul and higher forces have no judgment about such things. Only your ego experiences judgment. Since every soul experiences the same lessons and balancing, there is no reason to take your experiences personally and feel bad about yourself for having a particular experience. Only your ego does this.

In truth, your experiences—the good ones and the bad—mean nothing about you except that you are like everyone else. The ego likes to tells stories when it doesn't get what it wants, such as, "There must be something wrong with me" or "Maybe I did something bad in another lifetime" or "I will never be happy." The ego feels bad and persecuted or punished, but these are just stories, with no truth to them.

You have to learn to not tell yourself such stories. They'll keep you entrapped in the egoic state of consciousness when the lesson is to discover the Truth, which is that, in spite of your difficulty, you can be happy and, more importantly, you can become a better human being as a result. Your soul chose this experience for a very good reason.

Everyone has the same types of lifetimes on Earth or some other third-dimensional planet; everyone has the same curriculum. As you move through this curriculum, your experiences are unique, but everyone needs certain experiences as part of their soul's growth. Everyone at some point is a murderer, and everyone at some point is murdered. Everyone at some point is a pauper, and everyone at some point is a prince or princess. To learn all the lessons your soul has set out to learn, you need to experience every role. And, throughout all of your lifetimes, you grow and you are loved no matter what you choose.

If you are having a lifetime or period of physical difficulties or limitations, then that's the right experience for now, and you have to get on with getting the most soul growth out of this experience. How do you do that? You summon all of your best qualities, for that is how those qualities are developed—by exercising them. To become the best human being you can be, you must be what the ego is *not*. You must be humble, accepting, compassionate, sensitive, kind, gentle, patient, persevering, strong, and loving.

That is ultimately what you are here on Earth to do: to become those things, not what the ego wants you to become. There are lifetimes where you are meant to become what the ego wants you to become, because that experience is also valuable to the soul. And there are times when you are meant to develop the qualities of your divine self. Lifetimes of disability or significant illness are such times. Understanding this will help you accept your situation, and this acceptance will open the door to spiritual growth and transformation.

Lifetimes in which you experience illness and disability may be challenging, but they are challenging for a reason, and the gifts that are developed and the rewards of those gifts are great. They are the greatest treasures. What if you were able to see your illness, disease, or disability as a great blessing and a gift?

Many in this situation have come to see their difficulty this way. This is possible, and if you are struggling with health issues, this is your task. Transforming any bitterness, self-pity, victimhood, resentment, or anger into acceptance, humility, love, compassion, patience, perseverance, and strength is the true healing.

Healing doesn't always look like a healing of the body, at least not at first. Often, what must come before physical healing is a healing of the heart and mind. By this I mean that something *inside* you may need to change before you receive the physical healing you are praying for. The challenges in this life are meant to change you—to transform you—or they wouldn't be necessary.

Consequently, any challenge you're experiencing is right and honorable. It is the right experience, and it's helpful to see it this way. This is the first step in healing: Realize that you (and others) are having the right experience. That will allow you to relax and better receive the help that's being given you from higher dimensions and otherwise.

Whenever you pray for help, you will receive help in changing whatever incorrect beliefs you may be holding that are contributing to your difficulty and your suffering, which in turn, will transform your emotional state, since one's beliefs result in emotions, and those emotions are often behind any physical ailments.

What you are transmuting is what all human beings must eventually learn to transmute. Your task in this life is to learn to hold true beliefs—ones that align with love and cause your actions to align with love. Learning to love is the lesson of all your human incarnations. Everyone must walk this path of transmuting negativity into the positive emotions of love, joy, compassion, peace, courage, patience, and every other positive virtue that you know in your Heart to be true.

If you are unwilling to undergo such transmutation, that's fine. You can take as long as you need to recognize that you are love, for that is what all healing is about. Physical ailments and, indeed, all that ails you stem from a need to transform something within you that limits your experience of yourself as love. Pray for assistance in this transmutation, and healing of some kind will eventually follow.

My point is that healing doesn't always look as you wish or might expect, and it often takes time. But continue to sincerely pray for healing, and you'll receive the help you need to transform. You'll either receive relief from your physical issues or be more able to live with them because something inside you has changed. This transformation is the one your soul is trying to bring about through the limitation you're experiencing.

Consequently, praying to be healed physically might not be the right prayer, although it's certainly fine to pray for that. But be sure to also pray to learn what your soul wants most to learn from this experience. Pray to be transformed. Pray for inner strength. Pray for acceptance. Pray for insight. Pray for patience. Pray for your egoic tendencies to be healed. Pray to learn to be happy within your circumstances. Then, whether you are physically healed or not won't matter.

How do you make this leap, from resistance and unhappiness about your condition to surrender and welcoming the growth that can come from it? Prayer is the first step, and we on higher dimensions will do our work. Then, you have to do *your* spiritual work, which largely involves examining what you are saying to yourself that's making you unhappy with your situation. Granted, it isn't easy to be happy with your situation if you're having physical challenges. However, I'm not asking you to be happy about it, but only to see how your own thoughts are making it more difficult for you to accept your situation and carry on as best you can.

How are your thoughts undermining your happiness? How are they scaring you? How are they making you feel like you're missing out or lacking or victimized by this situation? None of those feelings are necessary, and when such feelings are no longer part of your experience, your situation will become much easier to accept and to bear. What are you telling yourself that makes your situation difficult to accept and to bear? This is very important inquiry work.

Every situation is made difficult by the voice in the head. That is its job—to create a sense of having a problem or a sense of lack, including a sense that *you* are lacking. This is literally the egoic mind's job. The voice in your head is the challenge in the experience of being human. It is the challenge that must be overcome by the hero or heroine for the hero or heroine to succeed. Just this voice.

I'm glad to say that this is all you have to overcome to stop suffering, although this might not bring much relief, since this may seem like a mighty task—to not believe what you believe, because that is essentially what I'm asking you to do: Don't believe your own thoughts.

How do you get from believing the voice in your head to not believing it? I will tell you the most efficient way: Learn to meditate, which the next chapter addresses. There is a way out of entanglement with the voice in your head, and the most efficient way is meditation.

Inquiry is another powerful means for pulling the plug on the power and momentum of the voice in your head, because once you see that your own mind is causing you to suffer by telling you half-truths and lies, you won't be able to continue to believe the voice in your head. Once a lie is seen, you can't go back to believing it. The trick is that you have to be aware of what you're thinking before you can see that it is false.

That's where meditation comes in. Meditation trains you to be aware of what you are thinking. However, anyone with enough motivation, even without meditation, can become more aware of what they are thinking once they realize this is important. So, if you want to become free from suffering, then make an effort to notice what you're thinking as you go about your day or when you're just sitting quietly, whether that's in meditation or just looking out the window.

Become aware of what you are thinking or what you just thought. Notice yourself thinking. What is it that notices this? What notices? And what thinks? Is there a thinker, or is there just a noticer of thoughts? These are important questions to ask yourself as you begin to become more aware of your thoughts.

The answer may surprise you, as you may discover that you are what notices thoughts and that what appears to be a thinker is simply an idea about yourself as someone who thinks the thoughts in your head. The thoughts that run through your mind are experienced by you, but if you examine this, you can see that you didn't think them into existence. Rather, they just appeared in your mind. From where? From nowhere, from the unconscious mind, which is the repository of conditioning.

Your egoic mind, the voice in your head, is programming, which is stored in the unconscious mind and released into your conscious mind as an ongoing stream of thoughts. Your thoughts are programming, just ideas stored within you and released rather haphazardly into your mind, where you identify with them and believe them to be *yours*.

The thoughts that make up the voice in your head aren't actually *your* thoughts but humanity's thoughts: thoughts that your ancestors thought, thoughts that your family members thought, thoughts that those around you thought when you were growing up, and thoughts people believe today.

Your unconscious mind is like a sponge that soaks up beliefs it has encountered through various people and the media and beliefs it's come to believe as a result of personal experience, many of which are incorrect conclusions. The voice in your head is an accumulation of all the beliefs you and others have held throughout time that still linger in your unconscious mind and the unconscious minds of those you are in contact with.

Some of these beliefs are true or somewhat or sometimes true, some are occasionally or only a little bit true, and some are not the least bit true. But because they show up in your own mind, the tendency is to automatically accept them as what *you* believe. This *you* is the false self. It's made up of beliefs that you think you believe because they show up in your mind for one reason or another. I'm not talking about any facts you may hold in your mind but all the stories and half-truths your mind tells you about you, others, life, and God.

The voice in your head wouldn't be a problem or cause any suffering if it were wise, helpful, and always true, but it is rarely this. Instead, the thoughts that run through your mind perpetuate the suffering that has gone on for as long as human beings have been alive. These beliefs are responsible for human suffering, and until you see that they are not true, they'll continue to create suffering within you, and you'll continue to pass those beliefs on to others.

What you wake up from when you have a spiritual awakening is the illusion and delusions cast by all the stories and half-truths that make up the voice in your head. The way out of this mass delusion that humanity has fallen prey to and the suffering caused by holding mistaken beliefs is simply to see that most of your beliefs about yourself, life, and God are not true, simply because they don't tell the whole truth, the whole story. You need to be humble enough to see that you've been wrong in believing so many things. The voice in your head assumes it knows so much, while it knows very little.

Seeing the truth about the voice in your head is especially difficult to see when those around you don't see that they also have been duped by the voice in their heads. No one is teaching you the truth about your thoughts, except some spiritual teachers who have awakened. You've been taught the opposite. Most people are unaware that they are the one causing their own suffering by what they are thinking.

To most, this is a radical idea, but it's time for more people to see this now. It is imperative to see this now, as humanity must come to its senses before more damage is done to each other and to the planet. Raising consciousness is largely a matter of seeing the truth about your own thoughts and then learning to detach from them so that they no longer affect you negatively. There is another way to live, and you are reading or listening to this because you are ready to live in this new way, and meditation will be your most trusty tool in this transformation. But there is one more…

Transmissions

There is another very important means of healing that we on other dimensions offer, which is important for you to be aware of because it is extremely beneficial and available for the asking. It's something I've spoken about extensively and which I and the other higher-dimensional beings working with me are involved with. I've written about it in *Faith, Facts, and Fiction: Finding Your Way on the Spiritual Path,* so I will include an excerpt from there, which will help round out this chapter on healing:

Transmissions have been used throughout history in various spiritual traditions to raise consciousness. Those who've attained a high degree of spiritual development naturally emanate and channel higher energies to those willing and able to receive them. These energies may be blocked by a negative entity in someone's energy field, but most people who open to these energies will receive them. The physical healings that I performed when I was alive were examples of a transmission of energy. Although not all transmissions result in physical healing, transmissions bring many other benefits.

This phenomenon has been observed around spiritual teachers, gurus, and other awakened or enlightened people for as long as there've been such people. These individuals generally abide in a higher state of consciousness than most, and when they're with others, they tend to raise the vibration of those around them. This just happens. And when those who are awakened or enlightened intentionally convey this higher vibration to seekers, and seekers are open to it, the transmission is even more effective.

Transmission is a fact. It has been observed time and time again throughout history. It is predictable and has consistent results. That predictability makes it a fact. Transmission is a true, observable phenomenon, and if you had the instruments, it could be measured.

The effects of transmission are numerous and depend, in part, on the intentions of the transmitter and receiver. Healers tune into and channel nonphysical beings who specialize in physical healing, while spiritual teachers use transmission primarily to raise consciousness. For this, spiritual teachers also receive help from nonphysical beings but ones who specialize in raising consciousness or who have a particular interest in assisting that teacher. When awakened teachers offer transmission to others, as long as their motives are pure, they'll receive help from higher-dimensional beings who know exactly what someone needs and how to facilitate each person's spiritual evolution.

Everyone has particular guides assigned to them. Healers and spiritual teachers and every other profession have guides that assist them in their work. No one really does anything by themselves. Creativity, inspiration, inventions, new ideas, information, healing, and transmissions come *through* people; they're not produced by people themselves. The human self is but a vehicle for expression of the Divine on earth.

You are never alone but always working with unseen forces on other planes, nonphysical beings who cherish your existence and want you to be happy and fulfilled. They're ready to supply you with everything you need if only you open to them.

Learning to open and receive is an important lesson on the spiritual path. To receive, it's important to trust that nonphysical forces exist and are available to help you. This is the truth. Without this trust and openness, you won't be able to receive as fully as possible from them. With this trust and openness, your life will become easier and greatly improved.

Sometimes, channeled information is not trustworthy, but don't let this fact stop you from opening to higher-dimensional beings who are available to assist you personally in your spiritual evolution through transmission and in other ways. If channeled teachings help you relax and experience the love, joy, and peace of your true nature, then you know you've come across the Truth.

The Truth has a positive impact on you on every level: energetically, emotionally, and physically through relaxation, as well as spiritually by uplifting you to a more loving and peaceful state. This is how you know Truth. If the words of a spiritual teacher or channel don't have this effect, then you probably don't need that information. So much channeled information is useless and unverifiable. Much of it doesn't improve your life but only feeds the imagination.

"The Truth will set you free," while falsehoods will imprison you in confusion, doubt, fear, and other negative feelings or simply keep you spinning around in your mind. These are signs that you've fallen prey to your own egoic mind or someone else's, and you don't need those thoughts or beliefs. Let this be your guide.

I came to bring peace and love to your beloved planet, and this is how it's done—by giving you the Truth. This Truth is apparent in your Heart, the spiritual Heart. It knows the Truth when it hears it, and it shows you this by bringing you into a place of relaxation, peace, and love.

The most obvious effect and essential purpose of transmissions is to raise your consciousness, or vibration. What do I mean by this? Simply put, transmissions shift you temporarily and eventually more permanently from the egoic state of consciousness to Presence, your natural state. They take you from identification with your false self to your divine self, and from human suffering to peace and love, which is your natural state.

The natural state is not a spiritual experience or state that you can't function in but the state that you are meant to function in. It is your optimal state, which is a state of contentment with life just as it is and a feeling of being in the flow, with no complaints or resistance to life. Awakening refers to a more permanent shift to your natural state as the default, which is what transmissions aim to accomplish.

Transmissions accomplish this by infusing you with a higher vibration of energy, which I and many others call Christ Consciousness. It is the consciousness of an enlightened one. While receiving a transmission and right after, you're uplifted to this level of consciousness or some degree of it. As a result of a transmission or a series of them, it's not uncommon to fall periodically into Christ Consciousness seemingly for no reason at all. It may be only for a brief second or longer, but this marks a process that will continue to grow if you open to it and make room for it in your life.

Christ Consciousness is a very ordinary experience, really. It is still, peaceful, compassionate, accepting, content, and loving. It's a feeling of upliftment, expansion, lightness, subtle joy, and ease. This consciousness resides within you, but it may not be experienced by you until it's activated by someone who abides in this state, either a person or a nonphysical being.

The process of embodying Christ Consciousness begins with getting a taste of Christ Consciousness through transmission. As you become more familiar with this state through transmission, you gain more and more access to this state yourself. This is a new way of being in life. Being able to abide in this state is the goal of the spiritual path and the hallmark of someone who's well established on the path.

Another benefit of transmissions is the healing of old emotional wounds and other limiting conditioning or patterns. Higher-dimensional beings help you release fears, buried emotions, negative self-images, untrue beliefs, and other conditioning that keep you tied to the egoic state of consciousness. During or after a transmission, people often experience a flood of tears, indicating a release of emotions. Tears may also be a sign of one's heart opening and being filled with love or devotion to God. These are tears that feel very good: cleansing tears and tears of upliftment and love.

One of the most important long-term effects of transmissions is a lightness of being. You may feel like a weight has been lifted from your shoulders. Finally, you are unencumbered by old images and ideas. Like being born anew, life seems immaculate, fresh, and full of possibilities. This is the experience of your divine self freed of the false self and its burdens. You find yourself laughing more, having fun, being playful, and being able to take yourself and others less seriously. Things don't bother you as they once did, or much less.

This lightness is what people are looking for and do expect from the spiritual path: an easing of the burden of being human, being able to see the bright side of life, loving life, and feeling good and at one with life. The spiritual path does result in this, and transmissions speed this along exponentially. They are a gift and a blessing, and one of the main ways that spiritual growth is accelerated, and with very little effort. All that's required is your openness and willingness to receive what has always been available to you and to everyone.

Physical healings can result from transmissions as well, especially if a transmission is designated specifically for that. You can always ask for a physical healing, and you'll receive whatever is in your highest good to receive. The problem is that it isn't always in your highest good to receive a healing when you're asking for one.

Illness and disability serve the soul's growth and deliver many lessons that can't be learned any other way, or at least not as efficiently. An illness or disability may also be making room in your life to do more spiritual discovery. Often, people have to be taken out of their routine before they'll take the time to go deeper spiritually, if that's the soul's desire. If you're experiencing physical difficulties, then that's the right experience for the time being, and you have to find a way to make the best of that experience.

Although instantaneous healings sometimes occur as a result of a transmission, what's more likely when you request a healing is that you'll receive insights or guidance intuitively that will speed your healing along by helping you learn whatever you need to learn from your physical issue. Often, something has to shift inside you before the physical difficulty can ease, and transmissions will help with that.

Transmissions uplift and connect you with your Source, with love, peace, and goodness. For this reason, they are pleasurable and beneficial. Feeling connected feels good and is good! The truth is that you are intimately connected to everything that exists in the physical world and beyond. You are connected because everything comes from the same source. God is alive within you and within all life. You are God made manifest in form! Everyone longs to experience this connection, and transmissions fulfill this. This is one of their functions.

Are transmissions dangerous? Let me begin by saying that transmissions *can* be dangerous. A lot of things can be dangerous, even very dangerous, such as fire, electricity, and riding a bike, but you still use or do these things because they're of benefit or enjoyable. So, a better question is: What makes transmissions dangerous and how can those dangers be guarded against?

What makes transmissions dangerous is the same thing that can make channeling dangerous: not being able to connect with higher-dimensional beings. The spiritual advancement and purity of the transmitter is the most important qualifier, since that will determine the level of energy they can transmit. Can they transmit Christ Consciousness? If they aren't awakened or enlightened, they probably can't, at least not consistently or powerfully.

Unless channels or transmitters are sufficiently advanced and purified, they'll reach all manner of beings with their own agendas who aren't suited to guide, help, or heal anyone. Negative streams of energy can come through psychics, channels, healers, and spiritual teachers if they're not spiritually developed enough or if they're driven by a desire for power, admiration, or wealth. After being in their presence or receiving a transmission from them, you're likely to feel bad or unsettled, and this negative state or even depression can linger for some time.

More importantly, transmissions from a negative source can stir up unconscious material that isn't meant to be stirred up, which may be difficult to handle. There's a time for everything, and some things are better off left alone. Stirring up repressed emotions prematurely may cause emotional problems. Transmissions from negative sources can also activate and misdirect kundalini, the energy that guides the spiritual process.

This is very different from the healing or spiritual process that is set in motion during a transmission from higher-dimensional beings, who know exactly what's needed and what someone is able to handle and how to facilitate that. Once higher beings set a process in motion, they stay with that person throughout the process. Long after the transmission, they remain connected to them and continue to work with them and support them during this process as best they can.

This is very different from what goes on when lower beings are involved. They may set a process in motion and then leave that process unattended. They often don't know what they're doing or don't care what impact they're having. Some even cause harm intentionally.

Another problem that can arise if transmitters are connected to lower astral beings is entity attachment. When someone unknowingly opens up to receiving a transmission from a lower astral being, that person is inviting that being or beings to inhabit his or her energy field. Those beings are then able to remain close to that person and influence him or her negatively through the mind. Opening yourself up to transmissions from those who aren't connected to higher-dimensional beings can cause entity attachments that linger and cause emotional problems, such as self-hatred, rage, addictions, depression or other mental illnesses, or suicide.

I want to make a distinction between the harm that can be caused by transmissions in the ways I just described and the discomfort or difficulties that are a natural part of the spiritual processes that are often set in motion by a transmission of higher energies. Even beneficial transmissions can result in uncomfortable symptoms: sleepiness or sleeplessness; sluggishness or lethargy; weeping or fear or other emotions coming up; energy running through the body; and restlessness or an inability to focus or do mental work, to name a few.

These symptoms are common and normal during and after a transmission and will pass without needing to do anything about them. The best thing to "do" in these cases is to not be afraid of these symptoms, relax, and know that they're part of a natural process. These symptoms are signs that clearing and adjustments are being made in the subtle energy body. They're part of the process of healing, clearing, and raising your vibration and making it possible for you to hold more light in your subtle body.

However, if you're afraid of this very natural healing process because you think something is wrong, that will create unnecessary suffering. When these symptoms occur, it's important not to pathologize them. Spiritual process (i.e., the movement of kundalini) is mysterious and sometimes uncomfortable and even difficult. But if you can relax and trust that these symptoms will pass and that the experience is accomplishing something of value, the symptoms will be easier to endure.

All in all, when a transmission originates from beings on higher dimensions, most people experience pleasant and positive "symptoms": upliftment, peace, heart-opening, a flow of love, gratitude, a release, a shift in consciousness, a quiet mind. These effects may last for minutes, hours, or days. Whatever the symptoms, they are evidence of a deep, mysterious, and important spiritual process that's been set in motion.

Transmissions are a gift from God. They help heal people's emotional wounds and facilitate their evolution whether they're on the spiritual path or not, as long as they open to them. This is why I and others offer them. If you would like to experience our transmission of Christ Consciousness energy, more information about receiving them is on this webpage:

https://RadicalHappiness.com/faq

Chapter 6
Meditation

The Benefits of Meditation

Meditation is valuable because it strengthens one's ability to observe, detach from, and see the truth about thoughts and feelings, which frees you from the suffering they cause and heals the mistaken beliefs behind those feelings. Furthermore, when you gain some distance from the voice in your head, you begin to see that there's something much vaster and wiser than the ego available to run your life—the divine self—and it is content and in joy, awe, and wonderment of life. A regular practice of meditation will result in the happiness, peace, and contentment everyone longs for.

Meditation is the key practice that moves people out of the egoic state of consciousness into the experience of their divine self. It shifts your consciousness and aligns you with your divine nature so that you are expressing *that* in the world instead of your ego. You *become* your best self, your divine self, instead of your ego, and are more able to experience compassion, love, patience, and acceptance.

Meditation not only affects you while you're meditating, but how you are in your daily life. Over time, a practice of meditation will change your experience of yourself and of life and thereby change your life. It will bring you into a more positive inner state, one in which you are also in touch with your intuition and inner wisdom. This state is a very attractive one and attracts to you what you need, so life goes much more smoothly.

Meditation also promotes emotional healing. When you meditate, emotions may arise that were once repressed, such as anger or grief. When that happens, you don't need to do anything but allow the emotion to be there, experience it fully in the body, give it time to reveal itself, unwind, and naturally move on. These emotions just want to be fully experienced, and then they'll naturally dissipate. They are generally feelings you didn't allow yourself to fully digest, or experience, possibly because you were too young when they occurred and didn't know how to deal with them.

Fortunately, meditation is very easy to do, and I'll explain here what I think is most important for you to know about it so that you can make meditation a part of your life, if it isn't already.

How to Meditate

What's most important to understand about meditation is not so much how to do it, since it's really easy to do and there's nothing tricky about it, or even why, as long as you're convinced enough to do it, but how often. How often is everything when it comes to meditation. Meditation that you do only once in a while will only be so helpful, even if you do it for fairly long. What's important is that you meditate daily—at least once a day for forty-five minutes or more. The reason for this is that meditation is like training a muscle, and like muscles, meditation needs a regular workout or you get out of shape, in a sense.

What you're doing in meditation is training your brain to rest in another state, one other than the default state of consciousness, which is the egoic state of consciousness. To accomplish this, you have to spend time each day in a meditative state. Then, you stand a chance of making that state your default state, which is the goal of meditation.

A daily practice of meditation will make it possible to live in a much more relaxed and contented state: a state of Presence—and this *is* possible. Plenty of people do live this way, but they probably meditate daily and have made living in Presence a goal.

It helps to know what your goals are—what your values are. What's most important to you? For most people, getting things done is a priority, and when that's the case, time spent in meditation is seen as a luxury, as unproductive, time they don't have. But that isn't true at all. Meditation is a necessity, not a luxury, as it makes everything a person does more effective, more efficient, and more enjoyable. It ensures that the time you do spend doing things is well-spent, as the choices you make from a state of Presence will be determined by your inner wisdom, not the voice in your head.

Once you become a regular meditator, some of the things that now take up your time might fall by the wayside. Many of the things that people do with their time are not as worthwhile as they seem, and meditation helps you see this, as you spend more time doing things that bring you joy and less time doing things that are about getting something your ego wants, such as shopping or working out or chatting with friends or watching television or YouTube. Most people spend a lot of time each day feeding the ego and little time feeding the soul. Once this changes, you feel different inside, and your life will change for the better. Living from Presence is a different state of consciousness and the goal of the spiritual path.

The point I want to make is that daily meditation is necessary to change your brain state more permanently. Without daily meditation, the changes the brain needs to make to become established in Presence are nearly impossible or would take a great deal of time. Spiritual evolution is slow, and there are two things that will speed it up: meditation and transmissions. If you think that reading more books and absorbing more teachings will bring you the shift in consciousness you read about, then you're fooling yourself, for as important as teachings are, reading and listening to teachings will not change your brain, only meditation will.

So, briefly, I'll explain the basic technique of meditation. First of all, with meditation, it's important to be very comfortable so that you can meditate for an extended period of time without moving your body. This is more important than holding your body in an upright posture, as is so often recommended by yoga and meditation teachers. So, make yourself very comfortable so that you can rest in one position without moving. Reclining at a forty-five-degree angle, propped up with pillows in bed or in a reclining chair, will make it easier to meditate for an hour or more, which will enable your meditation to be much deeper.

Since meditation is essentially focusing your attention on one or all of the five senses, there are a few basic types of meditation. You'll need to experiment with each of them to see which one works best for you. They are:

Meditation on sound. Because you can't think and listen at the same time, listening is a natural and pleasant way of moving out of the mind and into the present moment. In a listening meditation, you focus on a particular sound, such as a bell, or on a piece of music, someone's voice in a guided meditation, a mantra, an affirmation, or a prayer that you repeat silently to yourself.

Repeating a mantra, which is traditionally a meaningful Sanskrit word or phrase, is a time-honored type of meditation. The mantra could be "Om" or "Om Shanti, Shanti, Om," or "Om Nama Shivaya." Another possibility is to choose your own word, phrase, or short prayer, something that is personally meaningful or resonates with you. Particularly powerful phrases are ones that evoke praise, gratitude, love, or simply relaxation.

Alternately, you can simply focus on the sounds in the environment as they arise. Listen to the sounds around you as if you are listening *for* something. Listening for something brings you into an attentive, alert, curious state of watchfulness.

Receive the sounds without mentally commenting on them. If you find yourself resisting a sound, such as a barking dog, notice that resistance and then bring yourself back to listening.

Alternately, listen to the silence in between the sounds and in between the thoughts. This silence isn't actually silent at all but has a certain sound. Also, notice how a sound emerges from this silence and returns to the silence.

You can also do a listening meditation to a beautiful, relaxing piece of instrumental music. Let yourself become fully immersed in the music.

Meditation on your breath. This is the most common type of meditation that's taught, but that doesn't mean it's superior to the other types of meditation or best for everyone. The best meditation is whatever works best for you personally.

Meditating on the breath is essentially a meditation, or focusing, on the sensations involved in breathing: Notice the feel of the breath as it enters your nose and leaves your nose. And, without changing how you breathe in any way, notice the movement of your chest and how the body breathes rhythmically in and out, effortlessly, softly, gently. If you find yourself thinking about your breathing, your body, or anything else, bring your attention back to the *experience* of breathing.

A variation on this is counting to a certain number on the in-breath, holding your breath for a certain count, and then exhaling to a certain count.

You can also try counting your breaths. Silently to yourself, count "one" on the in-breath, "two" on the out-breath, "three" on the in-breath, "four" on the out-breath, and so on up to ten. Then, repeat starting at "one." See if you can get to ten without losing your focus. If you lose your focus, start over at "one." This gives your mind one more thing to be busy with, which makes it less likely to wander.

One of the reasons meditating on the breath is such an effective way to meditate is that the breath and the mind are connected: When your breathing becomes slower and deeper, your mind becomes calmer and quieter. So, in addition to simply noticing your breath, you can also experiment with breathing more slowly and deeply and notice what effect that has on your mind.

Walking meditation. This is a meditation, or focusing, on the sensations involved in walking. Tai Chi, Chi Gong, and yoga, when yoga is done as a meditation, are other types of meditation similar to walking meditation that work well for those who are more kinesthetic and find sitting still challenging.

Meditation on beauty. Choose something beautiful in nature to look at and give it your full attention: a flower, a sunset, the breeze blowing through the trees, the clouds moving across the sky, or any other beautiful sight that has the capacity to capture your attention. Receive the visual impression and experience its impact on your being.

Alternately, move your gaze from object to object, without letting it rest on any one thing. This is an especially good practice for when you are walking in nature. Keep your eyes moving around your environment.

Meditation on energy. Those who are sensitive enough to feel the energy of the subtle body can meditate on these more subtle sensations by simply noticing them without doing anything about them, just noting them and letting them be.

Meditating on all the senses and subtle energy. This is a practice, usually done with your eyes closed, of simply noticing whatever you are noticing, whether it is a sound, a sensation, your breath, or subtle energy. You give your attention to whatever you're aware of and let your attention naturally move, as it will, from one sensory experience to another.

What's coming in through your senses right now? What are you experiencing? A sound? Warmth? Coolness? Air moving? Tension? Pain? Many sensations are likely to be happening at once. Notice them without evaluating them, commenting on them, or thinking about them.

When you do this meditation on sensing, what you realize is that your awareness naturally moves from noticing one thing to another. It moves from noticing a sound, to noticing a sensation, to noticing a thought, and so on. And, of course, sometimes awareness rests in one place for a while. *You* aren't doing this—your being is. In this meditation, you aren't controlling where your attention is going but simply noticing where it is naturally going—where your *being* is naturally directing it. The only thing *you* are doing is allowing awareness to go where it wants to go, and you're simply noticing that and enjoying that.

This type of meditation is also a good way to stay anchored in the present moment as you go about your day. During your day, make it a habit to pay attention to what you are sensing rather than to what you're thinking.

The basic instruction for all types of meditation is to focus as much as possible on whatever you've chosen to focus on: your breath, your bodily sensations, your mantra, sounds, energetic experiences, or what you're seeing. Inevitably, thoughts or feelings will arise, and when they do, notice them, and then put your focus back onto your mantra, your breath, the words in a guided meditation, the sounds in the environment, the sensations and energetic experiences in your body, or a combination of the above. Whenever you catch yourself caught up in a thought, gently bring yourself back to your point of focus. Eventually, you'll catch those thoughts when they first arise before you get caught up in them, in which case, you notice any thoughts as they arise and then return to focusing on whatever you are focusing on.

The instructions for how to meditate are no more complicated than that. What's hard about meditating is doing it regularly and for long enough in one sitting to shift your consciousness. It takes most people, especially beginning meditators, forty-five minutes or more before they drop into a deeper state. You'll know when you've dropped into this state because it feels a certain way, which is difficult to describe, beyond calling it a shift. Once this happens, stay in that state a while, the longer the better. At that point, you may be able to drop your meditation practice and just experience the state that the practice has taken you to.

To quit meditating before you drop into that deeper state will undermine your practice of meditation because meditating won't be as rewarding. Once you are able to drop into this state more quickly and easily, you'll find yourself looking forward to meditating, and then making time to meditate each day will be much easier. But first, you often have to make meditation a priority and make a commitment to doing it daily for forty-five minutes or more before it becomes a joy. Many people give up on meditating simply because they haven't stayed with it long enough and done it frequently enough to make it rewarding.

I would also like to add that there's no such thing as a bad or failed meditation. Every effort you make to meditate is worthwhile and matters, whether you're aware of any results or not. Try not to hold goals in regard to your meditation, such as having a particular spiritual experience or developing in particular ways you've heard about from others. Meditation will change you in ways that may not be readily apparent. Spiritual progress is a mysterious thing, and the mind isn't able to assess or evaluate one's progress. The mind loves to tell the story that you aren't making any progress, so why continue? So, watch out for the ways your mind might try to discourage you. Of course, the mind doesn't want you to meditate.

Those guiding you in other dimensions are aware of your efforts to meditate, and these efforts signal them that you are committed to your spiritual growth. When they see your commitment to meditate, they'll concentrate more of their energies on helping you with your spiritual progress.

Please do not underestimate the involvement of spiritual forces. Know that when you set aside time to meditate, you draw to you assistance from other dimensions. They are assisting you in healing and elevating your consciousness.

So, be sure to ask for their help before you start meditating. It's always helpful to say some sort of prayer that expresses your sincerity to heal and progress spiritually and one that calls forth help from other dimensions. Meditation is a time for becoming closer and more connected to those who are guiding you. Know that they are there supporting you in your efforts and ask them for help when you feel you need it.

Overcoming Resistance to Meditation

The biggest hurdle to meditation is the egoic mind's resistance to it—and those are just more thoughts to notice and then turn away from. Don't let your mind talk you out of meditation, because your mind, of course, doesn't want you to meditate. What you're doing when you meditate is quieting the mind, and that's the last thing the ego wants. If you don't learn to quiet it, the voice in your head will take you on a ride, at best, and at worst, be your tormentor.

When faced with meditation, your mind will tell you, "This isn't working," "This is too hard," "I don't have time for this," "You'll never be able to do this," "This is boring," and anything else that might work to keep you from meditating. But every moment spent meditating is worthwhile, whether it seems like it or not. So, know that. The egoic mind isn't equipped to assess these things nor is it unbiased in its views of meditation.

When faced with meditation, the voice in your head has one agenda—to keep you from doing it. Fortunately, you just need to be aware that this is going on and not fall for the voice in your head's tactics. Meditation is not hard. It's enjoyable, in fact, and the best thing you can do for yourself on every level.

What I'd like to share with you next is a portion of a talk this author gave a while ago about overcoming resistance to meditation:

Gina: "I can't tell you how often people tell me how difficult meditation is for them and that they just can't meditate or they just don't want to. You'd think I was asking them to run a marathon or give me their first-born son. Resistance to meditating can be so strong! So, I feel I need to counter it with a reality check: Is it really so hard to sit still for an hour and listen to the sounds in the environment or to beautiful, soothing music or to a voice gently talking to you? Or to be still and just sense your breath or whatever else you are sensing?

The fact that meditation may still seem unpleasant even when I put it this way, points, I think, to how very restless our minds and bodies are and how much we are accustomed to filling up our every moment with doing, particularly doing driven by our minds. How often do you or most people just sit and do nothing—*just be* without getting lost in some form of media? Do you ever just sit and stare at the clouds or watch the breeze in the trees for more than a few seconds? When I was a child, my parents believed in just letting me lie in the hammock or stare out the window or sit on the patio. My dad used to spend hours just sitting on the patio in the summer by himself, doing nothing in particular.

Today, most of us schedule every minute of our lives and our children's lives with activities. This is considered normal and healthy, and yet, we all yearn for peace and quiet and nothing more to do on our to-do list. But yearning for this never gets us there. We have to go against our conditioning and make a conscious choice to *just be*. We have to value *just being* enough to actually make time for it—put it on our to-do list, or we will never take the time.

Meditation is an opportunity to put *just being* on your to-do list and discover the enormous and important benefits of doing so. We need to *just be* as much as we need food, water, air, and exercise. *Just being* is basic to our well-being. And it is crucial if we are to keep the ego in check and discover and begin to live more as our true self.

The things that people want most in life—peace, happiness, contentment, love, and wisdom—are cultivated and made available to us by taking time to connect with our being-ness. Ironically, what we all want most is not achieved through doing as much as being. Then, being informs our doing, and we use our time wisely and beneficially.

When we let the ego run us, which is what it does, we often put our energies in directions that are unnecessary, unproductive, or unfulfilling. You just may become *less* busy if you meditate, because certain activities will fall away, as they are seen as not worthwhile or not something you really want or need to do.

Meditation will change your life, but you have to do it regularly. What will it take to commit to this? What stands in the way of committing to it? What thoughts or beliefs might undermine your progress in making meditation a part of your life? I guarantee that if you make meditation a priority and do it an hour a day, it will change your life.

So, again, I ask you, "How hard is it, really, to recline in bed and focus on music or the sounds in the environment or your breath or a mantra or any of the other possible things you might focus on in meditation? Isn't it just the mind that "thinks" it's hard.

Even if it does actually feel difficult when you are just sitting and being, then that's an opportunity to notice what that experience is like. That's what meditation is about anyway: Notice whatever you are noticing and let it be. This is the practice. Notice, accept, and let it be. This is how you gain mastery over your mind, and that's what meditation is about and why it will change your life. You will become the master of your own life, or rather, the mysterious Self that is who you really are comes to the forefront and lives your life. Life lives through you.

Meditation is truly the answer for a better life and a better world. Believe this, trust this, and this belief will carry you through any rough spots or resistance."

Inquiries to Overcome Resistance to Meditation

Here are some inquiries you might find helpful in uncovering and dealing with any resistance you may have about meditating and being present:

1. How do you (your ego) feel about meditating regularly? What does the voice in your head say to you to keep you from meditating? And when you're meditating, what thoughts come up to try to take you away from meditating or discourage you from continuing?

It can be especially helpful to jot down the kinds of things the voice in your head says to try to keep you from meditating or to cut your meditation short. Writing them down helps you really see what the ego is up to and will also weaken the power these thoughts have over you.

When such thoughts arise, notice them and don't respond to them. They aren't really your thoughts but your ego's.

Recognize that they are ploys on the part of the ego to get you involved with your mind and not meditate. You are what is aware of the thoughts going through your mind.

2. Do you believe meditation is valuable? If not, how do you convince yourself that it isn't? If you don't believe meditation is valuable, then you probably won't do it. What do you value? People tend to take time for what they value. Given that, what does what you do with your time and energy say about what you value? Does what you spend your time doing reflect what you really want?

Notice how the mind devalues meditation. Notice how else the mind might undermine your commitment to becoming freer, happier, and more trusting of life. The mind often drives people in directions that aren't worthy of their time and energy with shoulds, guilt, fear, and desire.

3. Notice how uninterested the mind is in the present moment. The mind is fascinated with the past and the future, and it likes to evaluate the present, but the mind finds little of interest in the actual experience of the moment. Notice how persistently your mind makes suggestions for thinking about something or doing something other than just being in the moment and responding to whatever is coming out of the moment. The egoic mind has a job to do, and that job is to keep you from being present in your life.

How does your mind attempt to keep you out of the moment? Which tactics are the most successful at getting you to turn away from being in the moment? A memory? A fantasy? A desire? A fear? A should? A judgment? A thought about food, sex, time, work, what you have to do, imperfection, being successful, or how you look? How long do you actually stay in the present moment before you go unconscious and rejoin the egoic mind?

If you'd like to learn to meditate and make meditation and other spiritual practices part of your life, Gina offers a self-directed online course called Awakening Now, which you can begin any time. More information is on this webpage:

https://RadicalHappiness.com/online-courses

CHAPTER 7
Spiritual Practices Important to Healing

In this chapter, I'd like to present some key spiritual practices, all intended to shift your state of consciousness and raise your vibration. While meditation is something to do daily as basic spiritual hygiene to train your brain to live in a higher state of consciousness, the practices in this chapter are tools you can use to heal yourself more permanently of any negativity.

The Practice of Forgiveness

Forgiving yourself and others allows you to forget the past, to leave those memories behind and to live in the present moment. Forgiveness allows you to leave the false self behind and just be present as your divine self. It frees you from identification with the stories that create the false self and hold it in place.

Bringing the past, particularly unpleasant or traumatic events, into the present moment through thought doesn't serve. The aspect of mind that does this is not the rational part of the mind but the primitive part. In fact, going over traumatic or difficult events in your mind reactivates any wounds and tends to hold any wounding from the past in place. Remembering such events keeps the pain going and often delays the lesson that is meant to be learned from that experience.

Although you aren't in control of a memory arising, you can choose to not dwell on those thoughts. "Forgetting" the past in this way, by not dwelling on it, is part of forgiving the past.

Leave the past to God. It is not for you to regret the past or hold grudges or feel whatever you might feel as a result of the past. Give those regrets, grudges, resentments, anger, and even your self-righteousness toward those who have wronged you to God so that you can be free of their burden and be in life in love and peace. Let the past go, give it to God, and be in peace now. Many of you have carried the burden of the past long enough. You can drop it now and be free and at peace.

Forgiving Yourself

Sometimes, you will fall short of your spiritual goals and ideals: You will not be loving, you will not be compassionate, you will not be patient, you will not be tolerant. You will gossip, lie, exaggerate, judge, blame, and get irritated. You will falter. But once you see that you've faltered and accept that, the slate is wiped clean. You are forgiven, and you can begin again.

Forgiveness is automatic as soon as you see that you've made a mistake. The seeing of the mistake *is* the forgiveness. Accepting that you made a mistake will allow you to forgive yourself and move on. You are always forgiven, but if you don't forgive yourself, you'll stay stuck in the ego. Accepting that you made a mistake and that doing so is human allows you to forgive yourself.

If you have a negative tendency, such as judging or gossiping, do your best to not indulge in this. But if you do, acknowledge that you've made a mistake, accept that, have compassion for this human tendency, forgive yourself, and ask others for forgiveness if necessary. To judge or berate yourself only keeps you separate from your divine self.

A Practice

Make a list of those who have hurt or harmed you as well as those you have hurt or harmed. Go down the list and state this sincerely and wholeheartedly:

"I forgive you, I forgive myself for the ways I've contributed to the situation knowingly or unknowingly, I ask your forgiveness (if needed), *and I forgive myself for any negativity around this that I have harbored, and I thank you for the experience and lesson we created for our mutual growth."*

Really take some time with this exercise, as it has the potential to free you from your past. Forgiveness is something you do for yourself, for others, and for the whole world.

Also, do this forgiveness practice whenever a thought of someone comes up for whom you feel some ill-will or anger or a need to ask for forgiveness. Then, drop all thoughts about this person and the past.

Here is a prayer you might like to include in your forgiveness practice:

"Help me release this person and forgive the past. I am open to healing and completion around this relationship, and I surrender it into God's hands. The situation now unfolds perfectly for the good of all." Then, send blessings and love to that person.

Note: The above forgiveness practice was adapted from Jeffery A. Martin's Finder's Course Protocol.

An Inquiry

If you're having difficulty forgiving someone, ask yourself what forgiving that person means to you: Do you think it means you are weak? Or that you are condoning what was done? Or that the offense will be repeated? Do you feel that forgiving someone who did something wrong isn't right? Does forgiving someone mean you are "going easy" on that person and that he or she won't learn some lesson? What assumptions or beliefs do you have about forgiveness that keep you from forgiving?

Another way of asking this question is, what does it mean if you don't forgive? Does it mean you're being just and doing the right thing? Does it mean you're taking care of yourself? Does it mean you're in control and in power? Does it mean you're being strong? Can you see that there is, in truth, no good reason to not forgive, that any reason you come up with for not forgiving stems from the ego? Not forgiving bears only unhappiness, separation, and more negativity, and that's proof that it isn't in alignment with your divine self.

What is the result of not forgiving? Really take a look at both the payoffs to the ego of not forgiving and the negatives to your state of mind and to your relationships. What toll has not forgiving taken on you and your relationships or on others?

Forgiving and Letting Go of the Past in Relationships

The ego keeps a tally of every hurt and offense and everything the partner didn't do that he or she was expected to do. When the tally mounts up, the ego exacts its payment through demands, anger, or withholding. This only increases the pain in a relationship, often resulting in the other person retaliating or withholding. Forgiveness sets the scale back to zero so that the relationship can pull itself out of this downward spiral and have a fresh start.

Without forgiveness, resentments and anger pile up and kill love. A lack of forgiveness keeps you focused on the partner's failings or faults or on some incident. It keeps you in the grip of your emotions and at odds with love. Without forgiveness, your ego remains in power in your consciousness, and it will continue to judge the partner and look for further justification for its anger and resentment.

Without a willingness to forgive and forget, a relationship can't endure; or if it does, it will be miserable. Forgiveness allows you to drop back into your Heart, and it allows others to do that also. You forgive others because you value love, peace, and happiness more than you want to feel right or superior and more than you want to punish someone. You forgive because it feels good to forgive, because it feels better than being right, superior, angry, hurt, or sad.

You may think that if you forgive someone, you are being a doormat. But forgiveness puts you back in your power—back in alignment with your divine self. It doesn't take your power away. The ego saps your power with its negative emotions. Such emotions are a place of disempowerment, ineffectiveness, victimization, or cruelty. Negative emotions take your happiness and love away and give you nothing in return. Forgiveness is the gift you give yourself, which gives you back your happiness, peace, and love and brings love to your relationship again.

Once you are committed to forgiveness, then forgiving someone for something isn't any more difficult than committing to not thinking or talking about what happened in the past unless it serves your relationship to do so. Most thinking and talking about what happened in the past is in service to the ego and its agenda to punish the other person, to feel right and superior, or to play the martyr or the victim.

If thinking or talking about the past doesn't serve your relationship—doesn't enhance the love between you—then turn your attention away from thoughts about the past when they arise and put your attention elsewhere. After practicing this for a while, these thoughts won't come up as often, and they'll be less charged when they do. Eventually, you'll be free of that negativity. Negative feelings have never done anything for you, and they don't have to be part of your life.

Gratitude Practice

One of the most powerful tools for happiness and for awakening is gratitude. It is the antidote to the ego's dissatisfaction and sense of lack. The ego is responsible for that nearly ongoing feeling that something is missing, lacking, or wrong. Gratitude is a practice of seeing the glass as half full instead of half empty.

Gratitude is a matter of acknowledging what *is* here instead of focusing on what is *not* here. What *is* here is real; what *is not* here, such as how you would like it to be, is not real. When you go about your day, notice what you *do* have: what resources *are* here, what support is here, what love is here, what beauty is here, what peace is here. A practice of gratitude is noticing what *is* and being grateful for that.

Gratitude is also the way out of discouragement, despair, and every other difficult emotion. When you focus on something you're grateful for, all negativity disappears, because gratitude, since it is a quality of your true nature, puts you in touch with all of the other positive qualities of your true nature, such as joy, love, peace, and contentment. Once you step out of the ego's point of view, you feel the love, wonderment, awe, and gratitude of your true self for this gift of life. This is why it's so important to learn to detach from the voice in your head—because your life *can* be experienced as a blessing, as a precious gift.

Even in this moment—right now—it's possible to feel this simply by stopping to notice the love, joy, peace, and gratitude that are here right now. Just take a moment right now to do that, to see if you can experience any of those positive states right now, no matter how subtle.... Noticing the subtle experience of these positive states is something you can do at any time during your day, and the more you do this, the more you'll become established in these states.

So, what might prevent you from doing this practice? Wouldn't it just be a thought? If a thought is keeping you from taking time to notice gratitude, love, peace, or joy during your day, then just notice that thought, and then turn away from it and turn your attention to the experience of this sweet moment. Stay with this experience long enough to feel the subtle happiness of your true self in your body. Can you feel it, even just a little? The more you allow yourself to feel this, the more it becomes your reality.

Through a gratitude practice, you can learn to feel gratitude throughout your day for the wonderful little things in life that are such a gift and so often taken for granted by the ego. No matter what's going on, there's always something to be grateful for. In fact, there's always a lot to be grateful for. To shift from non-gratitude to gratitude, all you need to do is stop focusing on the mind's complaints and start focusing on what's showing up in life that you *do* like.

Gratitude opens the Heart and makes all other qualities of your true nature accessible. The feeling of gratitude is a feeling of happiness, love, and peace. The fact that you can create these positive feelings by simply noticing or naming what you're grateful for makes the practice of gratitude a very handy and powerful tool for your transformation.

It takes very little time to notice or name what you're grateful for. When practiced daily, this can become a way of being in the world. Instead of giving your attention to the thought-stream, try noticing and naming what you're grateful for throughout your day, and this will change your life. A potent formula for happiness is to replace thinking about yourself with gratitude.

A Practice of Focusing on Positive States

During your day, when you experience gratitude, love, happiness, peace, or any other positive state, stop for a few moments and focus on it. Let yourself sink into it. Really experience it and also notice how that state feels in your body. Hold your awareness, or attention, on the *energetic experience* of these positive states in your body for a few moments. Doing this will help you become more established in this state because it creates new neural pathways. These states represent the joy and excitement that the being that you are feels in simply being alive. Let yourself really feel that.

The Practice of Smiling

One of the bodily expressions of happiness is a smile. Did you know that you can create happiness simply by smiling? When you "put on a happy face," you become happy! So, if you're feeling stressed-out or unhappy, smiling will help you shift to a more relaxed and happy state.

Try smiling when a negative thought or feeling arises and notice how it shifts you away from negativity. Smiling sends a message to the brain that all is well and fight or flight is unnecessary. Did you know that even just imagining yourself smiling or seeing someone else smile makes your brain light up as if you were smiling?

Increase the amount that you smile. Some suggestions for doing this are smile while you're walking in nature, smile while you're driving, smile while you're at home doing your chores, and smile when you're listening to someone. Your smile doesn't have to be a big one to make a difference in your life. Even just a slight Mona Lisa smile, which Buddhists call an "inner smile," accomplishes this change in the brain. Many statues and pictures of the Buddha show him smiling this way.

Also, try smiling at yourself in the mirror for 1-2 minutes every day. As you're doing this, notice any thoughts and feelings that arise. Just be aware of them, welcome them, and let them be there, and keep smiling and sending love to your beautiful self.

The Practice of Sending Love

One very helpful practice you can do if you aren't feeling loved or loving, or anytime you find yourself stuck in the egoic state of consciousness is to send love. It doesn't even matter who or what you send love to. The act of sending love to *anything* frees you from the prison of the egoic state of consciousness. Sending love works, in part, because you can't do this practice and be identified with your thoughts at the same time.

The practice of sending love is simply a matter of intending that love be sent somewhere and holding your attention on that for a moment. Whenever you find yourself caught up in your thoughts, for instance, try sending love to them. Then, send love to whoever or whatever is in your environment, and this will bring you more firmly into alignment with your divine self. And, of course, at any time, you can send love to those who are at a distance or those who have passed away. Sending love to those you're struggling with is a particularly powerful and healing practice. Doing this will open your heart and heal your relationship.

Sending love works because it aligns you with the divine love within you, which helps you realize that you are love and you are lovable, and that others are as well. When you are in the egoic state of consciousness, you don't feel loving because you don't feel lovable, and others don't seem very lovable either. When you feel this way, it's a sign that your heart is closed. A closed heart makes attracting love and assimilating any love you do receive from others difficult. Sending love is a remedy for this.

One of the rewards of giving love is that you feel good about yourself. The Catch-22 is that if you don't love yourself, then being loving toward others is difficult. Somehow, this vicious cycle has to be broken, and a practice of consciously choosing to send love to others can do that, even if at first you aren't experiencing love when you do this practice.

The more you practice sending love, the more you feel worthy of receiving love. And the more worthy of love you feel, the easier it is to give love. And the more you give love, the more people love you and want to support you in various ways.

What you put out into the world is returned to you. If you put love out into the world, you'll receive love and so much more back. "Seek first the kingdom of God, and all else will be added to you." Give love, and all else will be given to you.

What people discover when they give love is that it isn't receiving love and the other benefits that love draws to them that makes them happy as much as the act of giving love. This is an amazing discovery! Giving is where the "juice," the joy, is. Giving is what feels good. What a surprise!

The ego believes the opposite of the Truth, so it really shouldn't be a surprise to discover that the truth is the opposite of what the ego believes! This is why "the truth will set you free." It sets you free from the ego.

So, here is how to do the practice of sending love. This practice may seem esoteric, but it is absolutely something anyone can do. To send love:

- Think of a person, pet or other animal, plant, or thing you want to send love to. Or notice a thought, feeling, or sensation that you might send love to.

- Then, connect with the subtle experience of love within your being.

- Next, intend that love be sent to whatever you've chosen to send love to and hold your attention on this intention for a moment.

- Imagine or feel the love energetically flowing from you to whatever you've chosen to send love to for a few minutes.

The purpose of sending love is to transform your consciousness and that of others. The effect that sending love has on your own consciousness will affect everything around you, and sending love specifically to someone else affects that person directly. Energy follows thought. It goes wherever you intend it to go. If you send love to someone, his or her energy body registers that, even at a distance.

Human beings are made of energy, and you are affected by each other's energy in beneficial and not so beneficial ways, whether you are conscious of that or not. Most people aren't sending a high vibration of energy to others—love—but something more like the energy of lack, fear, or anger. Fortunately, the energy of love can be consciously directed to others by you for the good of all if you intend that.

Buddhists have a wonderful practice of sending love to others by reciting, "May all beings be happy" and variations of this. Wishing others well is a powerful prayer. Doing this aligns you with your divine self and with love and uplifts others. Feel free to make up your own prayers or statements of this nature and use them.

Giving love to others by sending them love, wishing them well, or praying for them makes you happy and makes it easier for others to be happy too. When you give love in these ways, you are summoning guiding forces to help and protect others, and they come forward to do this. Your good intentions matter, not only to your state of consciousness, but to others. Your goodwill—love—is an actual force in the world. You can be either a force that is in service to love or one that works against love. You decide. Please choose to make this a better world.

More About the Practice of Sending Love

Lester Levinson, who was the originator of The Sedona Method™, used the technique of asking, "Can I change this emotion to love?" to heal his physical body and become enlightened. Here is more about his technique and some other exercises for you to do that will help you clear your relationships and enhance your ability to love. These are simple but powerful techniques.

1. Make a list of those closest to you, including those who've been the closest to you in the past. When you look at a name, notice what thoughts and emotions arise. If it isn't love, ask yourself, "Can I change this emotion to love?" Stay with this until the emotion changes to love. If you need to, consciously generate and send love to that person until love is the only emotion that remains. If you aren't sure how to get the feeling of love going, try recalling a memory of when you felt loving, and then transfer that feeling onto the person.

When you do this technique, you'll probably realize that you, and only you, are the cause of those thoughts and feelings and that those thoughts, and only those thoughts, create the experience of that person. So, be with those thoughts and feelings inside yourself, accept them, and take responsibility for them. Then, love will be able to flow.

2. As you go about your day, when negative emotions or negative memories of someone arise, ask yourself, "Can I change this emotion (e.g. anger, resentment, judgment, hatred, bitterness, blame, despair) to love?" Stay with this until the emotion changes to love.

3. Send love in meditation: In your meditation, spend at least 15 minutes sending love to everything that arises: a thought, a sensation, a sound, a pain, a feeling, an energetic sensation, and so on.

Note: This section about Lester Levinson's teachings was adapted from Jeffery A. Martin's Finder's Course Protocol.

A Guided Meditation for Experiencing Who You Are

Settle into wherever you're sitting or lying for now, and let yourself relax and take some nice, slow, deep breaths and just listen as I speak with you and as we explore together more deeply what it's really like to be alive here and now. It's time to set down all of your thoughts and all of your worries, and all of your concerns and just listen. All you have to do right now is sink further down into wherever you're resting, feel the heaviness of your body against whatever you're resting on, and just listen, listen with your whole body, not just your ears.

Listening with your whole body is what your Being does. It listens and uses the entire body to take in everything that's going on in this moment, things you would never have noticed if you were lost in thought. There's an entire world—and entire life living itself here and now in this very real, present moment, where you are just here, listening with your entire body.

You know what I mean by this, because this is your natural state. As I said, your Being is always listening, taking in life, registering it, but without any commentary or evaluation. That is the difference between the mind and your Being. It takes in what it's experiencing and experiences it fully without evaluating it or trying to hang on to it or push it away. It says yes to whatever happens to be arising in any moment. It loves it. It's curious about it. What will be next!?

Like this moment, for instance, what's arising now besides the sound of my voice? Another sound? A sensation? A thought? A feeling? An intuition? An urge to do something? …. And now?... All of life comes out of the moment, fresh and new, and you never know what that will bring. If a thought arises, that usually gets you involved in thinking, in the virtual reality of the mind. The same doesn't happen with sensations or sounds. They don't take you into another reality. They are reality. But if a thought arises, it often takes you into another world—the world of the imagination. Thoughts are special this way. They are a ticket into virtual reality. One thought, and you're instantly transported.

Just for now, let's stay here in this world of the here and now, this world of the senses, the simple experience your body is having, and see what you might experience. If a thought shows up, just notice that and return to noticing what else is here besides any thoughts you may be having.

What is actually here, now? What is real? If you think of anything that isn't actually here, then just let that go for the time being. We're going to explore reality, just as it is right here, right now, without thoughts. This will be primarily a sensory exploration, since the senses are all you have to experience reality. You have five senses and a sixth sense, which includes intuitions and other subtle perceptions. If you get caught up in a thought, no problem; just return to experiencing whatever sounds, sensations, subtle energies, or intuitions might be showing up. Notice how rich the Now is, how full it is of things coming out of it. Let's just rest here, now, and see what the next few moments are like. (2 minutes)

And now I want to tell you a little story about yourself, about who you really are, because you can experience this so much better when you're relaxed and resting like you are right now. I know it seems as if you exist as whoever you say you are when you describe yourself to others or to yourself. But that's just a character you're playing, like a costume with a mask and a script. You're all playing your part perfectly, just as you were meant to.

Some characters are happy, some are sad, some are fiery, and some are shy. But beneath all that, the same energy animates each of you. The energy that enlivens you, that makes it possible to move in all the ways you move, is exactly the same in each person. It isn't even different flavors or colors of energy, but exactly the same energy. What makes you unique is the costume and mask you wear. Nothing else. Without that, everyone is identical.

I'm not saying you're all alike because you are human. I'm saying that you're wearing a human costume, and underneath that costume, you are the same energy, and that energy isn't human or anything else you can put into words, which is why I'm just calling it an energy. That word fits because energy moves. It's always changing. The energy that enlivens you is alive. It gives life and it is life.

Did you know that you are life? Can you, for just this moment, feel the life force within you? It's what moves your body, it's what breathes your body, it's what sees and hears and smells and tastes and feels. This life force is who you are, and it's right here, right now. You are immersed in it, like a fish in water, so close that you don't even notice it, and yet it's what allows you to notice everything.

This life force is not contained in anything. It isn't contained in your body or in your cells. It moves within your body and your cells, but it is everywhere else as well. It has no boundary. This life force that is you exists everywhere and in everything. But when it's focalized in a human body-mind, it's experienced as separate from and distinct from itself, but it is not separate or distinct. It is in full contact with itself as everything.

What is this mysterious thing called life? It is God. This energy, this life force, is none other than God. God is not a Being or a human or a god but a force: life itself. If you wish to personify it, that's fine. People do this to relate to it. That's natural. But, still, God, this life force, is not an entity, and it certainly isn't a human entity.

You are not human! You're pretending to be human. You're playing the part of a human being, and this is why you suffer. If you knew yourself as the life force, you wouldn't suffer. So, this is what we're about here, peeling away the human costume some so that you can see what's really there. What's animating you? What is experiencing your life?

This word "what" gives the impression that this animating force is an entity. But how else can this question be asked? Language comes from the human mind and expresses the human experience. How can language express the truth about life, when it was created by the human character and its mind? It can't.

So, I'll be silent for a moment and let you just experience whatever you're experiencing. Again, this word "you" is very misleading, because "you" aren't experiencing anything. You could say your human character is experiencing, but this character is just an idea of about who you are dressed in a costume. What is really experiencing life is a mystery, and you don't need to understand that with your mind, and you can't.

All you need to do now is just experience, without any thoughts about that. Just allow yourself to have whatever sensory and extrasensory experiences come out of this mysterious moment. What are you noticing? That's all you have to do now is notice whatever you're noticing. So, let's do that for a few minutes: Start by noticing the sensations of your body touching wherever it's touching. Then, notice whatever sounds show up. Then, continue to notice anything else you notice. (2 minutes)

Now, as you continue to rest and experience whatever you're experiencing, just notice the space in which everything's arising. This space is empty. It has no shape, no color, no qualities whatsoever, and no boundaries. This space receives and allows everything that's happening without being affected or changed by it. This space is immutable and untouched by the comings and goings of life. It is fully accepting and allowing of whatever arises within it.

Now, just let yourself explore this space for a moment and see what it's like. Don't take my word for it. See for yourself what it's like. What is your body's experience of this space—not your thoughts about it—but your experience of it? How is your body experiencing it? How does your body sense it? If you tune in carefully, you might be able to experience an aliveness or vibration to this space, as if it were alive, which it is. The space in which everything arises is alive! And it's what gives life to everything: every sound, every sensation, every thought and feeling. Just rest in this space a while and see what it's like and what arises from it. (2 minutes)

You are this space, this life force: boundless, clear, spacious, infinite, pure, alive! This is God, and this is you, and this is everyone and everything else—just this empty, rich, intelligent space in which everything arises. Let yourself rest in this knowing now. It's the final and most complete knowing. You are it and you always have been.

The foregoing is one of the guided meditations in Gina's Deep Peace online course. More information about this course is on this webpage:
>   https://RadicalHappiness.com/online-courses/deep-peace-meditations

This guided meditation is also available to listen to on Gina's YouTube channel:
>   https://youtu.be/8q83TKzJ8OM

Make spiritual practices a part of your life, and you won't be sorry. By incorporating spiritual practices like sending love, smiling, focusing on positive states, gratitude, and forgiveness into your life, you will be able to maintain a higher level of vibration throughout your day. This world of yours is a difficult one. The vibration is very dense, and raising your consciousness also means raising the consciousness of others. You are not just waking up out of the ego for your own freedom from suffering, but also to uplift the consciousness of the world.

This is our purpose as well, for we wish only happiness and peace for you and your world. Please know that we are always available to you. No matter what state of consciousness you are in, no matter how low or desperate you might feel, just call upon us, and help is on the way. That is how benevolent life is. You are never alone. You only have to acknowledge that you know this by speaking to us, and we will be even more closely by your side, bringing you whatever you need for your healing. We are with you always.

ABOUT the AUTHOR

Gina Lake is a nondual spiritual teacher and the author of more than twenty-five books about awakening to one's true nature. She is also a gifted intuitive and channel with a master's degree in Counseling Psychology and over thirty years' experience supporting people in their spiritual growth. In 2012, Jesus began dictating books through her. These teachings from Jesus are based on universal truth, not on any religion.

Then in 2017, at the request of Jesus, Gina and her husband, who is also a nondual spiritual teacher, began offering Christ Consciousness Transmissions to groups online in weekly meetings and monthly intensives. These energy transmissions are a direct current of love and healing that accelerate one's spiritual evolution.

Gina's YouTube channel has over 250 messages from Jesus to listen to. Her website offers information about her books, online courses, transmissions, a free ebook, and audio and video recordings:

www.RadicalHappiness.com

Christ Consciousness Transmission (CCT) Online Weekly Meetings

Transmission is something that naturally happens from spiritual teacher to aspirant and from beings on higher dimensions to those who are willing to receive on this dimension. Transmission has been used throughout the ages to accelerate spiritual evolution and raise consciousness. In the process, emotional and sometimes physical healing also take place, as a clearing of energy blocks from the energy field is a necessary and natural part of raising consciousness.

In weekly online Zoom video meetings, Gina Lake and her husband offer Christ Consciousness transmissions. This is one of the ways that Jesus and the other Ascended Masters working with Jesus intend to raise humanity's level of consciousness. A channeled message from Jesus is given before the transmission to prepare, teach, and inspire those who are there to receive the transmission. Many report feeling a transmission come through these channeled messages as well.

The transmission takes around twenty minutes and is done in silence except for some music, which is meant to help people open and receive. During the transmission, Gina Lake and her husband are simply acting as antennas for Christ Consciousness, as it streams to earth to be received by all who are willing to open to and be uplifted by divine grace. Since there is actually no such thing as time and space, these are not a barrier to receiving the transmission, which works as well online as in person. You can find out more about these transmissions on Gina's website at:

www.RadicalHappiness.com/transmissions

Awakening Now Online Course

It's time to start living what you've been reading about. Are you interested in delving more deeply into the teachings in Gina Lake's books, receiving ongoing support for waking up, and experiencing the power of Christ Consciousness transmissions? You'll find that and much more in the Awakening Now online course:

This course was created for your awakening. The methods presented are powerful companions on the path to enlightenment and true happiness. Awakening Now will help you experience life through fresh eyes and discover the delight of truly being alive. This 100-day inner workout is packed with both time-honored and original practices that will pull the rug out from under your ego and wake you up. You'll immerse yourself in materials, practices, guided meditations, and inquiries that will transform your consciousness. And in video webinars, you'll receive transmissions of Christ Consciousness. These transmissions are a direct current of love and healing that will accelerate your evolution and help you break through to a new level of being. By the end of 100 days, you will have developed new habits and ways of being that will result in being more richly alive and present and greater joy and equanimity.

www.RadicalHappiness.com/online-courses

More Books by Gina Lake

Available in paperback, ebook, and audiobook formats.

Cycles of the Soul: Life, Death, and Beyond. What is the soul? And what is this human life all about? What happens at death and after death? What is it like in the afterlife, and do you plan your life before you are born? In this channeled book from Jesus, he answers these and many other questions. This wise and compassionate perspective from Jesus will help you embrace life and be at peace with life and with death.

A Heroic Life: New Teachings from Jesus on the Human Journey. The hero's journey—this human life—is a search for the greatest treasure of all: the gifts of your true nature. These gifts are your birthright, but they have been hidden from you, kept from you by the dragon: the ego. These gifts are the wisdom, love, peace, courage, strength, and joy that reside at your core. *A Heroic Life* shows you how to overcome the ego's false beliefs and face the ego's fears. It provides you with both a perspective and a map to help you successfully and happily navigate life's challenges and live heroically. This book is another in a series of books dictated to Gina Lake by Jesus.

Awakening Love: How to Love Your Neighbor as Yourself: "This book is what I would teach about love if I were walking among you today. It takes its organization from particular quotes of mine and others from the Bible, which have come down through time. The quotes this book is built upon are the core teachings I gave then and I offer you today. If they are adhered to, they will change your life and change your world." –Jesus

What Jesus Wants You to Know Today: About Himself, Christianity, God, the World, and Being Human: Jesus exists and has always existed to serve humanity, and one way he is doing this today is through this channel, Gina Lake, and others. In *What Jesus Wants You to Know Today,* Jesus answers many questions about his life and teachings and shares his perspective on the world. He brings his message of love, once again, to the world and corrects the record by detailing the ways that Christianity has distorted his teachings. He wants you to know that you, too, have the potential to be a Christ, to be enlightened as he was, and he explains how this is possible.

The Jesus Trilogy. In this trilogy by Jesus are three jewels, each shining in its own way and illuminating the same truth: You are not only human but divine, and you are meant to flourish and love one another. In words that are for today, Jesus speaks intimately and directly to the reader of the secrets to peace, love, and happiness. He explains the deepest of all mysteries: who you are and how you can live as he taught long ago. The three books in *The Jesus Trilogy* were dictated to Gina Lake by Jesus and include *Choice and Will, Love and Surrender,* and *Beliefs, Emotions, and the Creation of Reality.* Each of the books in the trilogy is also available individually, and they can be read in any order.

All Grace: New Teachings from Jesus on the Truth About Life. Grace is the mysterious and unseen movement of God upon creation, which is motivated by love and indistinct from love. *All Grace* was given to Gina Lake by Jesus and represents his wisdom and understanding of life. It is about the magnificent and incomprehensible force behind life, which created life, sustains it, and operates within it as you and me and all of creation. *All Grace* is full of profound and life-changing truth.

Made in the USA
Monee, IL
22 June 2023